Biblical Thinking for Building Healthy Churches

IX 9Marks Journal

I0163307

info@9marks.org | www.9marks.org

Tools like this are provided by the generous investment of donors.
Each gift to 9Marks helps equip church leaders with a biblical vision and practical
resources for displaying God's glory to the nations through healthy churches.

Donate at: www.9marks.org/donate.

Or make checks payable to "9Marks" and mail to:
9 Marks
525 A St. NE
Washington, DC 20002

Editorial Director: Jonathan Leeman
Editor: Sam Emadi
Managing Editor: Alex Duke
Layout: Rubner Durais
Cover Design: OpenBox9
Production Manager: Rick Denham & Mary Beth Freeman
9Marks President: Mark Dever
Paperback: 978-1-955768-97-9
eBook: 978-1-955768-98-6

EXPRESSIVE INDIVIDUALISM AND THE INTERNET

GENDER, SEXUALITY, AND EXPRESSIVE INDIVIDUALISM

ELDER MEDITATION: AN ELDER MUST NOT BE QUARRELSOME

Editor's Note

Jonathan Leeman

My friend Ben suggested that 9Marks should devote a Journal to Carl Trueman's book *The Rise and Triumph of the Modern Self* and the topic of expressive individualism. The elders of Ben's church, Capitol Hill Baptist in Washington, DC, had all just read it together and benefited from it immensely. I loved the book, too, and had told dozens of people to read it. I even emailed a friend at Crossway and told him they *had* to produce a teenager's version. Teenagers need to understand expressive individualism now, today, immediately, even more than adults, as they grow into a world suffuse with it. Still, a Journal on it? Nah, that couldn't work. Too philosophical, right?

Then Ben sent me a proposed table of contents. I thought, goodness, yes, we have something here. This Journal idea really could help pastors and churches. So I got on board, and we commissioned a number of articles.

Weeks passed. I began to wonder again, is this going to work? Isn't it all a bit abstract and academic? A topic like "expressive individualism" is just a mouthful to say, much less understand. It's not concrete like "Deacons" or "Doctrine" or "Church Discipline," which have immediate application to pastors.

Yet then the articles began to come in: Justin Harris on why pastors need to understand it, Michael Lawrence on how to apply sermons in light of it, Ben Wright on how it shows up in churches that love the nine marks, Walt Mueller on youth ministry, Samuel James on the Internet, and on and on. Goodness, yes, these are excellent. Pastor, not only will you enjoy these pieces, so will your elders, small group leaders, and anyone in your church who wants to better understand the culture we live inside, and that too often lives inside of us.

Think of Princess Elsa's song "Let it Go" from *Frozen* that all four of my daughters probably know by heart: "It's time to see what I can do / To test the limits and break through / No right, no wrong, no rules for me / I'm free!" Tim Keller helps define expressive individualism by pointing to these lyrics as

> a good example of expressive individualism. Identity is not realized, as in traditional societies, by sublimating our individual desires for the good of our family and people. Instead, we become ourselves only by asserting our individual desires against society, by expressing our feelings and fulfilling our dreams regardless of what anyone says. (*Preaching:*

Communicating Faith in an Age of Skepticism, page 134)

So what exactly is expressive individualism? It's a worldview, says Brian Rosner in a book he has just written on it (see the Journal Table of Contents for an excerpt), that he summarizes in seven tenets:

- The best way to find yourself is to look inward.
- The highest goal in life is happiness.
- All moral judgements are merely expressions of feeling or personal preference.
- Forms of external authority are to be rejected.
- The world will improve dramatically as the scope of individual freedom grows.
- Everyone's quest for self-expression should be celebrated.

Certain aspects of a person's identity—such as their gender, ethnicity, or sexuality—are of paramount importance. (Page 24)

Based on those tenets, my guess is, you know exactly what Rosner (and Trueman) are talking about. You see it all around you, too.

Understanding expressive individualism, therefore, is crucial for your pastoral ministry, just like pastors in the Roman world needed to understand paganism, pastors in the early twentieth-century needed to understand scientific materialism and rationalism, pastors in a Muslim world need to understand Islam, or pastors in East Asia need to understand Confucianism. The predominant religion in the West and many parts of the world today is expressive individualism. It shapes the religious intuitions of our non-Christian neighbors, our children, even ourselves.

The Lord's Prayer doesn't come instinctively to our lips. What Brian Rosner calls "The Prayer of the Authentic Self" does. Here is Rosner's rendition, which matches line by line to Jesus's prayer:

> My essence within,
> help me to find my authentic self,
> my kingdom come,
> my will be done,
> from birth to seventh heaven.
> Give me today my daily spread.

> Forgive not my enemies
> as I suppress those who sin
> against me.
> Lead me not into self-doubt
> but deliver me from all external
> authorities.
> For the kingdom, the power,
> and the glory are mine
> now and forever.
> Amen. (p. 209)

Pastor, this is how people in our world and too often in our churches instinctively, inarticulately pray. We hope this Journal will help you teach them to pray not to their essence within, but to "Our Father, who is in heaven."

And one more thing. We've decided to add a new feature to every Journal: to pick one elder qualification as listed by Paul in the Pastorals, and to ask several pastors to meditate on that qualification for all our benefit. For this issue, we decided to focus on what it means to be quarrelsome. In this social media moment, quarrelsome tempts all of us. Let's pick a fight with quarreling through prayer and meditating on God's Word.

Why Pastors Need to Understand an Abstract Topic Like "Expressive Individualism"

Justin Harris

I must admit: when I first came across Carl Trueman's new book, the title and the cover did little to entice me. What does "the self," "cultural amnesia," "expressive individualism," and "the road to the sexual revolution" have to do with the day-to-day things I face as an ordinary pastor? It all seemed so philosophical, so abstract, so obtuse. Nevertheless, upon the recommendation of a few friends and mentors, I took the plunge. Upon resurfacing from the book several weeks later, I was stunned to learn that every one of those philosophical topics shaped my life, ministry, and world more than I could ever imagine.

The goal of this article is to convince you of this as well.

THE DESPAIRING DIAGNOSIS

First things first: what's Trueman trying to say? Essentially, he argues that our current time and place is morally and philosophically unique. Similar to Aldous Huxley's dystopia in *A Brave New World*, but with one massive difference: in Huxley's fantasy future, the community reigned; in our modern world, the individual reigns. Put simply, the recent onslaught of the sexual revolution is merely a symptom of a new, individualistic world order.

Indeed, sexual sin has plagued us since the Fall. Yet, never has this expression of rebellion been so acceptable, thorough, widespread, and celebrated. Trueman illustrates the uniqueness of our time by contemplating the following sentence: "I am a woman trapped in a man's body" (*Rise and Triumph,* 19ff.). Think about the so-called plausibility of such a statement in our modern day. Biblically (and logically), we know this statement is preposterous. Yet for many, it makes sense. In fact, it makes *so much sense* to some that agreeing with it has become a matter of legal and societal consequence.

Twenty years ago, most people would have scoffed. That's no longer the case. And so, Trueman says, welcome to the sexual ethos of our brave, new world.

In the old world, Judeo-Christian standards of sexuality were largely understood and at least superficially embraced. Sexual sin and deviancy existed, but usually under the cloak of darkness (i.e., shame) or in abject defiance of the social order (i.e., rebellion). Now, however, a biblical understanding of gender, sexuality, and marriage is viewed with suspicion, if not all-out scorn. Simultaneously, sexual deviancy is considered normal, and perhaps even morally superior. The question is no longer, "How can anyone say he is a woman trapped in a man's body," but rather, "How can anyone *even question* whether anyone can say he is a woman trapped in a man's body?"

Put simply, the sexual revolution has triumphed. But … why? How did we get here? In answering these questions, the genius of Trueman's work begins to shine. He's not answering the question we maybe want him to ask: "How do we stop or reverse the sexual revolution?" Instead, he slowly traces the sexual revolution's triumph. Like a skilled doctor, he explains through the societal, cultural, and ethical symptoms to render an accurate diagnosis. And his conclusion will surprise you.

Pastors and church people alike would be tempted to think this is an easy answer. I can hear it now, "Class, what caused the sexual revolution?" The pastors and people yell out, "Sin!" But Trueman resists such simplistic answers. Blaming sin for the sexual revolution is like blaming gravity for the collapse of the Twin Towers.

To understand our brave, new world requires us to understand not only the gravitational force of sin but also the philosophy and political stratagems employed by it. He summarizes the main culprit in two words: "expressive individualism." This term refers to the tendency to find our meaning by giving expression to our own feelings and desires (46). Through careful historical and cultural analysis, the book traces the 300+ year history of the political rise of the self. At the risk of oversimplification, the devolution happened via three strategic steps.

1. First, through the influence of Rousseau and other post-Enlightenment thinkers and poets, the self became "psychologized." Who we were was no longer to be determined by our family, country, or church; instead, key thinkers and artists convinced us that we could and in fact must determine *who we are*. According to these propagandists, identity shouldn't be informed from anyone or anything outside of us, but created or expressed from within.

2. Second, through the teaching of Freud (with some scientific leveling of the playing field by Darwin), the psyche—that is, the internally determined self—became sexualized. As Darwin's theory reduced man to an elevated animal, Freud capitalized upon this by arguing that as a higher animal humans are essentially sexual. Though many of Freud's theories and practices are outdated and irrelevant, this insistence

upon mankind as a fundamentally sexual being has taken root in popular thought.

3. Third, and finally, through the surprising influence of Marx and other 20th century political progressives, the sexualized psyche became politicized. If the self is inherently sexual, then any denial or discouragement of certain rights and liberties is simply another expression of hegemonic oppression. Down with the traditional tyrants advocating for Judeo-Christian sexual mores, up with the newly liberated sexual selves who inherently deserve the right to enjoy their sexual appetites free from scorn or disapproval.

The sexual revolution didn't cause the sexual revolution. Rather, the rise and triumph of the sexual revolution owes its victory to the rise and triumph of the psychologized, sexualized, and politicized self. If churches don't treat the issue at this level, then they may be deceived into merely treating symptoms, never striving toward an actual cure.

THE DYNAMIC SOLUTION

So what's the cure?

Trueman admits he doesn't have many highly formulated answers. His "concluding unscientific epilogue" concedes that there's more work to be done here, although he does try to forecast possible futures within society and the church (383–407).

While it seems solutions could come from multiple quarters—the family, the arts, the academy, the political realm—there's one that cannot be neglected: the local church. This is precisely why 9Marks decided to devote a Journal to this topic. Whatever other solutions may be conjectured, time and thought must be invested in leveraging the one institution accompanied and empowered by the risen Christ (Mt. 28:18–20), the one entity against which "the gates of hell shall not prevail" (16:18). Specifically, it seems that healthy churches stem the tide of expressive individualism as they continue to leverage the authoritative Word and live out authentic Christian community.

Leveraging the Authoritative Word

Healthy churches unwind the errors of expressive individualism as they leverage the authoritative Word of God. In order to preserve our children and church members from the contagion of expressive individualism, we must steadily dispense the antiviral of biblical truth. In other words, our teaching must be marked by expositional preaching, biblical theology, and the gospel.

Expositional preaching, for example, deploys the authoritative Word against many erroneous ideologies. Whereas our culture tells us that truth is something one feels or something that looks appealing, expositional preaching is an actual argument from an objective, supernatural source—God himself. As the emphasis and shape of one's sermons consistently matches the emphasis and shape of the divine text, the congregation is reminded that truth is objective and authoritative. Furthermore, they're reminded such truth exists *outside* us.

Healthy churches will also abundantly disseminate *biblical theology* not only in the sermons but also in additional classes. First, let us consider biblical theology as the storyline of Scripture and then examine it simply as theology that is biblical (i.e., sound doctrine, systematic theology).

As church members regularly imbibe the redemptive-historical storyline of the Bible, the popular social imaginary obsessed with the expressive individual loses more and more sway. Scripture is indeed a story and at its center is not the self, but the sovereign and triune God. This story discloses not only who God is but also what he has done. First, he created gendered, corporeal human beings in his image to reflect his sovereign goodness throughout the universe. Sin of course ruined the divine ideal. And yet, God orchestrated a rescue plan for sinful rebels, thereby restoring them to forever fellowship both here and now in this fallen world and there and then in the new heavens and earth. In fact, though the hero of the story is the Savior, each act informs our understanding of the self.

This rescue plan is the gospel.

1. In the opening act, God creates human beings in his image to

reflect his sovereign goodness as they procreate, cultivate, and protect the created world from anything or anyone that would oppose God.

2. In the next act, sadly, human beings listen to the Serpent's promise of an enhanced self and disobey God. Though the self was cursed on account of sin, God deployed promise after promise to assure his people that he would destroy their enemy and restore to them the blessings they forfeited.

3. In the third act, God fulfills his promise by sending his Son to become a gendered, corporeal human as a new representative for the world. Though the first human, Adam, failed, Christ would succeed—obeying God's law perfectly, dying on the cross to satisfy God's fully righteous wrath, and physically rising again to declare his victory over the powers of death, hell, and sin.

4. In the fourth act, a new humanity enjoys spiritual life now and the promise of eternal physical life in the future as they depend on the person and work of Christ for rescue. Upon trusting in Christ, they are physically baptized and invited to partake of the Lord's Table whereby they are identified as part of the visible people of God.

5. Finally, in act five, the risen and still human, gendered, corporeal Son of God returns to rule with his embodied people over a new heavens and new earth for all eternity. Such a narrative is not only more compelling than anything offered by Rousseau or Freud, but it also has the advantage of being absolutely true.

In each of these acts, God exercises his sovereign grace over his physical creatures. As we teach this narrative, we defang the pliable and ultimately nihilistic notions of the self propagated by others.

Healthy churches ought to be a "pillar and buttress of truth" (1 Tim 3:15). This phrase assumes the protection and propagation of propositional revelation. In other words, local churches bear the unique responsibility to uphold sound doctrine. We must "contend for [all] the faith that was once for all delivered to the saints" (Jud 3), which means doctrines connected to anthropology may warrant special attention in our day. Now more than ever, churches need to fight for the truth and beauty of embodied existence and related truths such as the *imago dei*, complementerianism, gender, marriage, and sexual ethics. Trueman rightfully points out that Protestants especially have some make-up work to do: "Protestantism with its emphasis on the preached word grasped by faith, is perhaps peculiarly vulnerable to downplaying the importance of the physical. ... A recovery of a biblical understanding of embodiment is vital. And closely allied with this is the fact that the church must maintain its commitment to biblical sexual morality, whatever the social cost may be" (406–407).

As grateful as we may be for seminaries, denominations, para-church entities, and websites, the local church is still the "pillar and buttress of truth." Even if the gospel is "folly to those who are perishing," to those of us who are being saved it is still "the power of God" (1 Cor 1:18).

Living in Authentic Community

At the same time, healthy churches are more than proclaimers and defenders of gospel truth. Healthy churches also stem the currents of the modern self through their gospel community. Trueman shows the both-and nature of the church's charge, "If the church is to avoid the absolutizing of aesthetics by an appropriate commitment to Christianity as first and foremost doctrinal, then, second, *she must also be a community*" (Trueman, 404). This is true because the self is not merely understood from reading and study but through interactions with others around us (for more on this see pp. 56–59).

Consider, for example, the act of being baptized into membership. It's a remarkably passive act. One does not baptize himself or unilaterally "decide" to belong to a local church; rather, he must *be* baptized and she must *be* received into the fellowship of that church. In healthy churches, one cannot merely "identify" as a Christian; Christ has entrusted this job to his churches. In fact, one cannot even choose to remain identified as a Christian apart from the regular approval of a congregation; that's what it means for a local church to bear the authority and responsibility to excommunicate those who persist in unrepentant sin (Matt. 18; 1 Cor 5). Church membership and its counterpart, church discipline, draw a bright line between who belongs to Christ and who does not. And this strikes at the very heart of modern views of the self.

But the gospel community enjoyed in healthy churches is the result of much more than its formal structures. Healthy local churches not only make disciples by "baptizing them in the name of the Father, Son, and Holy Spirit" but also by "teaching them to *observe all things I have commanded* you" (Mt. 28:19–20). Once more, we do well to affirm the transmission of gospel content, but the goal of said content is *conduct*. Just as baptizing assumes the instrumentality of another, so does the teaching unto obedience.

In other words, Christianity is not a self-improvement project.

Healthy churches not only make disciples by marking them via the sign of baptism (initially) and Communion (ongoingly) but they also mature these disciples via the modeled, mentored, and interpersonal application of the Word. We grow not only by instruction, but by imitation (1 Cor. 4:16; 11:1). Therefore, healthy churches exhort their members to both grow in holiness and help others do the same. All of this directly confronts the modern notion of the self. Instead of the church member expressing himself, he is exhorted by others to die to self and mimic Jesus instead.

CONCLUSION

In many ways, ministry in the 21st century West really is the best of times and the worst of times. Some unhealthy churches have fully capitulated to the rise and triumph of the modern self. Others have effectively rebelled against its influence.

Let us conclude with the following hypothetical examples.

The less healthy the church, the less potent its impact. Popular sermons centered on felt-needs will likely only further fuel unbiblical notions of the self. For at least thirty years, evangelical churches have tried to create "community" around applicable sermons and personal affinities such as music, hobbies, or life-stage. Such churches haven't equipped people well to understand and confront the modern view of the self. In some cases, attractional churches not only fail to dampen the flames of expressive individualism; they fuel them.

On the other hand, imagine a church where God's Word is proclaimed and protected. Imagine gathered saints regularly being formed and shaped by the gospel, expository preaching, sound doctrine, and biblical theology. And imagine those same believers officially covenanting together as a Christian community, preaching the gospel to the lost, practicing the Lord's Table until he comes, provoking one another to godliness, and protecting one another from the errors and evils of sin. In a church like that, the self is minimized as the Savior is magnified. Yes, sin still frustrates and persists—and it will until the Lord returns. But until then, such churches will have a positive influence on a darkening and decaying world.

ABOUT THE AUTHOR

Justin Harris is the senior pastor of Faith Bible Church in Naples, Florida.

Do 9Marks Churches Foster Expressive Individualism?

Ben Wright

Few demographic tribes are more likely to "amen!" a critique of attractional church methodology than 9Marks readers. When attractionalism says, "We're offering the experience of worship that you're looking for," we 9Marksy types sniff danger. We believe congregations gather not to be offered a passive experience, but instead to offer worship as active participants.

"God, we thank thee, that we are not as other men."

But wait.

WE'RE ALL ATTRACTIONALISTS NOW

Carl Trueman teaches us how culture subtly shapes us. Five hundred years ago, everyone was a theist. Europe was overwhelmingly Christian, at least by nominal conviction. And to be Christian was to be Roman Catholic.

Today, within our array of denominational options, we find tribal subdivisions. There are "a host of other subjective variables—where we feel comfortable, welcomed, supported. We can choose our churches as we choose a house or car" (385). We then use the car we chose to drive past a dozen or more churches we didn't choose. Urbanization and modernization weakened our ties to close-knit communities and, then, handed us technology to sever those ties.

Can we assume that our tribe is immune to subtle influences from our cultural context? Is it possible that we anti-attractional types have unknowingly carved out an attractional niche of our own? What about our flocks?

Like many of you, I've heard more often than I care to remember the parting words from beloved members: "We love you and the church, but there just isn't enough X for me/my spouse/my kids." Sure, we try to learn from their feedback and make corrections as we're able. But have those parting words really exposed major misfires on basic biblical principles? Or are they often merely expressions of our departing members' personal feelings and desires—what makes them feel at home and comfortable?

To search for meaning by expressing our own feelings and desires, which Trueman calls expressive individualism, he also argues "is the very essence of the culture of which we are all a part" (25).

All of this crystallized for me recently when I read the resignation letter from "Jackson." He'd hate being identified with attractionalism. But his letter said, "As you know, I've been a supporter of [church-growth-critic pastor]'s ministry for some time. Over the years I've visited all the [church-growth-critic pastor] churches around town. We will be joining [names one of them]."

I realized that he was irresistibly attracted to a particular posture on complex cultural issues, a particular interpretation of difficult texts, and a particular emphasis in the pulpit ministry. And he knew where to find a church that expressed those preferences.

So I can't blame this brother for instinctively wanting a church that aligned with his preferred expression. And I can't really blame myself for not convincing him to agree with me.

But I do blame myself for missing the gravitational pull of expressive individualism on the hearts of serious Christians. They may not know it, but they're powerfully drawn to what makes them comfortable. That goes for me too.

WHERE TO LOOK FOR YOUR CHURCH'S EXPRESSIVE INDIVIDUALISM

Ask yourself: Excluding the biblical essentials, what draws your church members in? What keeps them around?

It could be the location, accessibility, or design of your meeting place. It could be your church's size—whether large or small. Or your "vibe"—your musical style, how people dress, your staging, your use of technology. It might be your posture toward government health guidelines or how exactly you respond to the latest story on cable news. And the children. Oh, the children—the number of kids, the age of kids, the space for kids, and the programs for kids. It could even be your distinctive style of expositional preaching.

Did you notice how many of those factors are closely tied to a church's expression of worship? Even those factors that don't show up on Sunday morning likely do show up in the life of our covenant community throughout the week. We may even leverage them to advance our disciple-making mission. But the specific expressions themselves are non-essential.

HOW EXPRESSIVE INDIVIDUALISM IS DAMAGING YOUR CHURCH

- It undermines missions. We should be sending mature believers. But often those mature believers rarely go overseas. Who knows why? Perhaps their affection for healthy church principles has become an obstacle that stifles our mission to send and go.

- It harms church planting. We plant churches because we perceive a need—often related to population growth, or the dearth of healthy churches in a particular area. That new church may not yet have many of the healthy planting church's attractive "options." Believers who should covenant with the new church may be disinclined if they don't find their preferred expression of corporate life and worship.

- It weakens rural churches. Our cars make it easy for us to drive from the country town of 5,000 to the suburb and its accompanying ecclesiological smorgasbord. As a result, small-town churches are weaker, less healthy, and less prepared to make disciples in their communities. Their unconverted residents are unlikely to visit healthy but distant suburban churches.

- It dilutes neighborhood presence. Inside a city, it's easy to travel through multiple neighborhoods to the church that matches our preferred expressions. A dozen faithful Christians in the same neighborhood might attend a dozen different faithful churches. And it's less likely that they'll partner to make disciples in their neighborhood.

- It undermines multi-generational and multi-ethnic churches. Since different demographic groups often prefer different ministry programs or expressions of style, they often sort into churches that reflect those preferences. We lose the energy, the wisdom, the maturity, the experiences, the long-term stability, and even the friction that a diverse congregation possesses. Perhaps more importantly, we limit our ability to reflect the heavenly image of all nations worshiping at the throne of Jesus.

- It intensifies ideological imbalance. We watched churches sort during our recent pandemic. We saw churches market themselves to capitalize on the moment. Many churches are now more dispositionally homogeneous. Sadly, many Christians found the group of people who   saw things the way they saw them. When the next crisis breaks up our new coalition, we can always re-sort.

As Jonathan Leeman puts it in One Assembly, there are unintended consequences to our churches' expressions both of our members' individual preferences and our pastoral preferences. He writes, "The devices of the marketplace aren't exactly conducive to encouraging people to eat in another guy's restaurant. You'll never see a McDonald's commercial celebrating their common cause with Burger King in solving the problem of hunger" (113). We've unintentionally undermined our partnerships with our sister churches and with the mission Jesus entrusted to us.

HOW TO FIGHT EXPRESSIVE INDIVIDUALISM IN OUR CHURCHES

Imagine one of your church's families moves to the exurbs 45 minutes away. Perhaps to their surprise, they find a pretty healthy church. Good preaching—expositional—but not polished. Plural elder leadership. Clear proclamation of the gospel. In the ballpark on, say, seven of the nine marks.

Now imagine the family doesn't like the vibe. Not many young couples. Almost no kids. An outdated nursery. Painful special music. Harmonicas make an occasional appearance.

Or imagine you pastor a rural church, and one of your families moves into the nearby city. The most 9Marksy church there talks about problems in its community like mental health and inequities in the criminal justice system. The family isn't used to this, and so they wonder if the church is progressive. If they're honest, both families would rather keep driving 45 minutes to your church.

Do you want them to?

My question for us is this: Are we shepherding our congregations now to make that decision well? Are we discipling the military family or the petroleum industry family to thrive in an English-speaking international church? Are we preparing them to use their gifts to build up a local church that's less mature than ours? Or are we unintentionally reinforcing their natural preferences—in other words, their expressive individualism?

Beware of whatever draws people to your church that's not biblically essential. What's trendy now will change. The demographics of your community will shift. If you're not careful, your members will be a shrinking pool of people who are committed to a particular set of antiquated preferences because you never discipled them *not to be.*

The better you nail a "vibe" that draws people, the harder you'll need to work to teach them that's not what they need most. The more your church's expressions of worship line up with what people instinctively like, the more you'll need to clarify that those non-essentials really are non-essential.

So, no—even if they've become essentials to some of your members—my solution is not to dump AWANA or the senior saints' excursions.

During the 1864 siege of Petersburg, Virginia, Union forces tunneled under one section of Confederate fortifications and blew them up. We call that episode the "Battle of the Crater", which the Union still lost.

You probably don't want a crater where AWANA used to be. You're not a general at war; no, you're an oncologist. You want to shrink the cancer, preserve healthy tissue, deftly separate the tumor from vital organs, and then remove it. The cancer is the tendency in your people—and yourself—to think we need our church to express what we prefer, what makes us comfortable.

When our comfort undermines our mission, it's an idol. Kill that idol. But save the body.

ABOUT THE AUTHOR

Ben Wright pastors Cedar Pointe Baptist Church in Cedar Park, Texas.

Summary of Carl Trueman's, *The Rise and Triumph of the Modern Self*

CULTURAL AMNESIA, EXPRESSIVE INDIVIDUALISM, AND THE ROAD TO SEXUAL REVOLUTION

John Benton

Washington Irving wrote the fanciful tale of a hen-pecked, work-shy man named *Rip Van Winkle*. Published in 1819, the story is set in late 18th century America and tells how Rip lay down while out squirrel hunting in the Catskill Mountains of New York. Dulled by drink, he fell into a deep sleep. He awoke 20 years later, not realizing that he had slept more than a night.

There were signs something strange had occurred. His beard was a foot long, his dog was gone, and his rifle was covered in rust. When he entered his village he didn't recognize it. There were buildings he didn't remember. His clothes looked old-fashioned. Children made fun of him. Rip proclaimed himself a loyal subject of King George III not realizing that while he had been asleep the War of Independence had occurred and America was now its own country. He was out of place and he didn't know why.

Many Christians today are having a similar experience. They may not have been physically asleep for 20 years, but they have maybe been cocooned in a little Christian bubble of Sunday church, Christian conferences, Christian books, and Christian music. They've been insulated against and disconnected from secular society. Now they're waking to the fact that the world has changed and things can't go on as they have before.

Believers used to be thought as somewhat odd but basically decent folk. Now we are increasingly regarded as a harmful influence in society. We're now "the bad guys."1 Things like freedom of religion and freedom of speech were once regarded as absolute rights. Now they're being challenged. You can lose your job for expressing certain ideas, especially biblical ideas concerning things like gender and marriage. Society is dramatically different—possibly in unprecedented ways. And it's likely to get worse before it gets better.

PASTORS IN A HURRY

As an example of how much things have changed, Carl Trueman begins his landmark book on this subject by asking how the statement "I am a woman trapped in a man's body" has somehow become cogent and meaningful in today's society.2 Our grandfathers would have heard such a statement with blank incredulity. But now it's supposed to be taken very seriously indeed. What has happened?

Trueman's *The Rise and Triumph of the Modern Self* is the most thorough and helpful introduction so far to our current situation. However, it's more than 400 pages of intensive thought and tightly argued argumentation. Many busy pastors simply will not have time.

So I want to give my own brief biblical introduction and attempt to sketch an overview of Trueman's work. My purpose is to get

1 See *Being the Bad Guys*, by Stephen MacAlpine, Good Book Company, 2021

2 *The Rise and Triumph of the Modern Self: Cultural Amnesia, Expressive Individualism, and the Road to the Sexual Revolution,* by Carl Trueman, Crossway, 2020, page 19.

us thinking and hopefully for pastors to be able to give accessible teaching on the situation to God's people. After all, this isn't simply a piece of fascinating contemporary history; it's something which may well cause faithful Christians to lose their friends and maybe their livelihoods.

PART 1: BIBLICAL BACKGROUND

Many cultural norms concerning sex and acceptable sexual behaviour have been swept away. In particular, the Christian view of gender and marriage is being rejected as oppressive and damaging (Genesis 1:27; Matthew 19:4–5).

How did we get here? First, we need to get a grip on this from Scripture. This seismic shift hasn't come out of nowhere, neither does it take the God of the Bible by surprise.

What Happens When God Is Rejected?

For the last hundred years or more, secular thinkers have argued that God either doesn't exist or at least is an irrelevance to daily life. He could be dispensed with and very little would change. But the Bible says otherwise. To turn away from God affects a society at the deepest possible level. We should understand that this is the root of the titanic changes we are witnessing.

I'll cover two key New Testament passages.

First, Paul's words to the church at Ephesus:

> They (those without God) are darkened in their understanding and separated from the life of God because of the ignorance that is in them due to the hardening of their hearts. Having lost all sensitivity, they have given themselves over to sensuality so as to indulge in every kind of impurity, with a continual lust for more. (Ephesians 4:18–19)

These verses spell out the trajectory toward hedonism for those who live without God. "Having lost all sensitivity" to God and to spiritual things, they fill the void left in their hearts with sensuality. They "give themselves over" to physical pleasures. Paul indicates that this heads in the direction of illicit sex, which will tend to extremes. This is where we are.

Consider also Paul's words to the church at Rome:

> The wrath of God is being revealed from heaven against all the godlessness and wickedness of men who suppress the truth by their wickedness, since what may be known about God is plain to them, because God has made it plain to them. For since the creation of the world God's invisible qualities—his eternal power and divine nature—have been clearly seen, being clearly seen from what has been made, so that men are without excuse.
>
> For although they knew God, they neither glorified him as God nor gave thanks to him, but their thinking became futile and their foolish hearts were darkened. Although they claimed to be wise, they became fools, and exchanged the glory of the immortal God for images made to look like mortal man and birds and animals and reptiles.
>
> Therefore God gave them over in the sinful desires of their hearts to sexual impurity for the degrading of their bodies with one another. ...
>
> God gave them over to shameful lusts. Even their women exchanged natural relations for unnatural ones. In the same way the men also abandoned natural relations with women and were inflamed with lust for one another. ...
>
> He gave them over to a depraved mind, to do what ought not to be done. (Romans 1:18–32)

Note the parallels between the passages. Paul speaks of those who have "given themselves over" to sensuality, but we also read that "God gave them over" to their sinful desires and appetites as an expression of his wrath for their denial of him. When God is denied society does not stay the same. It tends to become sexualized, and aggressively so.

This is our society, our current culture. In some ways, Trueman's book simply traces in modern history the trajectory indicated by these texts. The Western world used to be thought of as "Christendom," but it has now become dominated by sex and sexual politics.

Of course, there have always been libertines. But now their ideas command the culture. For centuries, a Christian morality and view of family has been a fundamental building block of Western society. But now that's being overthrown.

So, in this booklet we will try to summarize Trueman's work as to how this has happened and is happening and note some of his conclusions.

Preliminaries

Before we get into the argument, there are some preliminary ideas which Trueman has borrowed from other modern thinkers and to which he refers.

Mimesis and Poiesis

Here's how Trueman defines these terms:

> Put simply, these terms refer to two different ways of thinking about the world. A mimetic view regards the world as having a given order and meaning and thus sees human beings as required to discover that meaning and conform themselves to it. Poiesis, by way of contrast, sees the world as so much raw material out of which meaning and purpose can be created by the individual.[3]

Suppressing the truth of the Creator God and opting for no God at all invites us to Poiesis. We make of the world what we want with no one to tell us what to do. As Christians with an understanding of sin and the built-in rebelliousness of fallen human nature, we can see why people would naturally prefer Poiesis to Mimesis.

Three Types of Worlds

The American sociologist Phillip Reiff has a related idea. He spoke in terms of three types of worlds.

"First worlds" are pagan, with moral codes based on myths generally accepted by the society. "Second worlds" are those based on a faith in their God. Both first and second worlds, therefore, have a moral outlook founded in something transcendent, outside of people. This provides a source of stability for those societies.

By way of stark contrast, "third worlds" do not root their moral imperatives in anything sacred.

---

3 Trueman, 39.

There's nothing and no one above themselves. They justify themselves and their actions on the basis of themselves. Rejecting God moves us into what Reiff would call a third world.

In fact, Reiff labels this kind of third world an "anti-culture" because it sees the civilization and moral frameworks of first and second worlds as oppressive and restrictive of personal freedom. A third world deliberately attempts to destabilize and destroy first- and second-world cultural norms through what Reiff calls "deathworks." These are things which cynically make the old values look impotent and ridiculous. This is a primary aspect, for example, of pornography. Not only does it promote lust and treat people as mere "things," but it also repudiates any notion that sex has any significance beyond the pleasure of the act itself. God and those who want to restrict such pleasure are nothing more than prudish kill-joys.

In Reiffian terms, we now live in a third world, or at least on the brink of it.

PART 2: THE MODERN SELF AND IDENTITY

Dispensing with God has reshaped how people now think of themselves and of others. Trueman writes:

> The underlying argument is that the sexual revolution, and its various manifestations in modern society, cannot be treated in isolation but rather must be interpreted as the specific and perhaps most obvious social manifestation of a much deeper and wider revolution in the understanding of what it means to be a self.[4]

Trajectory of the Self

Trueman employs a few labels in order to summarize the historical pathway of the self. The "psychological self" was followed by the "romantic self." This was succeeded by the "plastic (or malleable) self." Next came the explicitly "sexual self," which has now, under the arguments of the New Left, become the "sexually politicized self." That's my paraphrase of his argument. I'll explain each below.

All these are quite different from what we might propose

4 Trueman, 35

as a biblical view of self, made in the image of God, fallen but redeemed. The Christian view of the self is an outward-looking self. We look to God and to Christ for our meaning and identity. But the modern self has turned inward.

The Psychological Self

Our first stop en route as we come away from Reformation thinking into the period of the Enlightenment of the 18th century is with Jean-Jacques Rousseau (1712–1778). For Rousseau, people are intrinsically good until they are corrupted by the forces of society. According to Rousseau, an individual's real identity is found in his or her inner psychological autobiography.[5] Rousseau wrote of his *Confessions*: "It is the history of my soul that I promised, and to relate it faithfully I require no other memorandum; all I need do, as I have done up until now, is to look inside myself."

Along with this went an emphasis on self-love,[6] empathy, and sympathy as the main informers of conscience and the tension between the individual and corrupt society. Trueman comments, "In Rousseau, we can see emerging the basic outlines of modern expressive individualism."

The Romantic Self

Poets of the late 18th and early 19th centuries—Wordsworth, Blake, and Shelley—take the ideas of Rousseau from the intellectual elite and popularize them into mainstream culture. Rousseau's idea of society corrupting and brutalizing the innocent individual seemed commonplace in the days of the Industrial Revolution. The solution was to turn both inward and back to an idealized, rural existence.

Trueman states, "Both Wordsworth and Shelley articulate views of poetry that press a clear connection between poetic aesthetics and ethics." True morality for these romantics was about what felt right and looked right. Once you look away from external frames of reference, all "moral" judgments tend to become nothing but expressions of personal preference or feeling. We enter a "therapy culture." This has major implications for sexual ethics. Authenticity as a human being is

---

5 Trueman, 129

6 Compare 2 Timothy 3:2

about being unashamed of one's own desires and acting on them.[7] Obviously, such thinking provides undergirding for much of what's going on today.

The Plastic Self

Plastic man is not simply psychological. He is, in Trueman's words, "a man who thinks he can make and remake a personal identity at will."[8]

The foundations for such thinking were laid by the philosophers Frederich Nietzsche (1844–1900) and Karl Marx (1818–1883), and by the scientist Charles Darwin (1809–1882). Nietzsche is famous for his grim atheism which saw life as a power struggle and invites us to rise above human nature and become Ubermench (overman). Marx saw industrial production and capitalism as not only changing society but reshaping people themselves and how they related to one another. Human nature is therefore plastic or malleable. Human nature is not merely a product of the times. It's not fixed.

---

7 Contrast Matthew 5:27–30 and Romans 8:13.

8 Trueman, 164

Darwin's account of human origins reinforced this. People must accept that they are mere accidents of evolution and therefore not made in order to fulfill any kind of destiny. He blurred the lines between the human and the animal and removed any idea of humanity having special status. We are ever-evolving. We are plastic.

The Sexual Self

Sigmund Freud(1856–1939), the father of psychoanalysis, is a key figure in this story. He equated happiness with "genital pleasure." This is the point at which personal identity became equated with sex and sexuality. Now that idea dominates the Western world—so people are categorized according to their sexual desires: gay, bi, straight, etc. For many, this is the most prominent truth about who they are.

If for Rousseau the natural man was innocent, for Freud the subconscious of human beings is dark, violent, and irrational. The job of the psychoanalyst was to excavate the unseen forces that live within us and bring them to the surface of consciousness. It's interesting that the inspiration for psychoanalysis was classical mythology (the

Oedipus complex, etc.)[9]. In his book *Selfie*, Will Storr cites an expert as saying "without the myths of ancient Greece … there would be no psychoanalysis."[10]

Freud places the sex drive at the very core of what it is to be human.[11] Before Freud, sex was for procreation and pleasure (Proverbs 5:19). Now it's who we really are. The happiest person is the one who is able to constantly indulge his or her sexual desires. However, this plays into the hands of powerful individuals, so we need civilization to curb this. So from a Freudian perspective, according to Trueman, "it means that it is impossible for the civilized to be truly happy."[12]

The Sexually Politicized Self

Freud's ideas were later used to change the classic understanding of oppression. This is another crucial move in the story.

Because identity is about our inner self, especially our sexual desires, then victimhood becomes psychologized. The idea that oppression is about poverty or physical mistreatment is eclipsed. It is, in this case, those who feel are unable to express their sexual desires, or whose sexual desires are deemed unacceptable by society, who are the oppressed. Oppression is about emotions.

Sex is no longer a private activity because it relates to our social identity. To outlaw or merely tolerate gay sex, for example, is to outlaw or merely tolerate a certain identity. It hits at the very heart of who a person believes themselves to be.

Many university humanities departments have adopted so-called "Critical Theory."[13] As a result, they have latched on to this new understanding of victimhood and oppression. The New Left interprets traditional sexual codes as a malicious strategy for maintaining the status quo in society.

9 2 Timothy 4:4

10 Storr, 113

11 It should be noted that if sex is at the center of what it is to be human then children have to be sexualized. This is where the agenda for sex education to be pushed earlier and earlier comes from.

12 Trueman, 219

13 Trueman summarizes the basic tenets of Critical Theory as follows: 1. The power can be divided between those who have power and those who do not; 2. The dominant Western narrative is really an ideological construct to preserve its own power structure; 3. The goal of Critical Theory is therefore to destabilize this power structure by destabilizing its dominant narratives that are used to justify it.

Western ideals must therefore be overthrown. According to this understanding, the family is the authoritarian state in miniature. And so dismantling the family is now thought by some to be essential for political liberation.

Sexual revolution is the way to achieve this. And this agenda is pushed even further by the philosopher Herbert Marcuse (1898–1979). Values such as tolerance are a sham, and simply a way of pacifying people to accept patriarchal, capitalist power structures. The fight must be against educational institutions that teach tolerance.

Identity and Community

Desire for inner happiness and psychological well-being lie at the heart of the modern era. As we've seen, it's now accepted that the way you see yourself, your inner image, is the true you. This even takes precedence over one's body,[14] which opens up the possibility of a difference between your biological sex and your gender. Who you think you are is your real identity, regardless of whether you have XX or XY chromosomes. Hence the statement, "I am a woman trapped in a man's body." It now "makes sense."

However, for one's identity to flourish, it must be acknowledged by others. The technical term is that identity is dialogical; in other words, it relies on language which is only developed through interaction with others.

Because we are relational beings, we need the acceptance of others in order to be comfortable with ourselves. This means that society must serve the purpose of meeting individuals' psychological needs. This then creates therapy culture in which all institutions and communities (including the church) must adapt to reflect a therapeutic and inclusive mentality.

Trueman reflects on this:

> The refusal by any individual to recognize an identity that society at large recognizes as legitimate is a moral offense, not simply a matter of indifference. The question of identity in the modern world is a question of dignity. For this reason, the various court cases in America concerning the

---

14 This means that theologically the modern outlook can be classed as a form of Gnosticism.

provision of cakes and flowers for gay weddings are not ultimately about the flowers or the cakes. They are about the recognition of gay identity and, according to the members of the LGBTQ+ community, the recognition that they need in order to feel that they are equal members of society.[15]

This explains why the faithful church is unlikely to be simply ignored. The Bible draws lines where current secular ideology wants no lines. As with so many other things in which we all fail, same-sex attraction and the confusion of gender does not fit with God's good creation. Therefore, in the long run, it will not cause individuals or society to flourish.

PART 3: EROTICISM, THE THERAPEUTIC, AND TRANSGENDERISM

Sex and sexuality now dominate the Western world.

In his book, Trueman highlights ultimately three "triumphs": how the erotic is pervasive in modern life, how especially crucial legal decisions are now made on the basis of emotivism and aesthetics, and how transgenderism has made headway in society.

Eroticism

From TV soap operas to teenaged pop music, our culture is now saturated with sexual themes.

The prevalence of pornography is especially noteworthy. Of course, technology has played a part. If freedom and happiness are encapsulated in sexual satisfaction, then online pornography becomes the obvious, the easiest, and the most private (it seems) medium of liberation and fulfillment. Pornography epitomizes the sexual revolution because it presents sex as merely recreational—a physical, pleasurable act that is divorced from any greater relational significance or transcendence. It detaches sex from any ethical context.[16]

And attitudes have changed. Pornography is no longer seen as an example of male dominance and violence against women. There's even talk of "ethically sourced" pornography, where

---

15 Trueman, 69

16 This is the impression given, even though pornography is often related to depression, suicide, and sex-trafficking.

women are not coerced to participate and the "rights of performers" are respected. Trueman writes,

> The philosophical claim I am making here is that the normalization of pornography in mainstream culture is deeply connected to the mainstream culture's rejection of sacred order. Pornography carries with it a philosophy of sex and of what it means to be human that is inimical to traditional religious perspectives, in the West's case primarily Christianity. It is therefore both symptomatic and constitutive of the de-created, desacralized world that emerges in modern times, with roots in Rousseau and Romanticism, and given sharp expression in philosophical and scientific idioms by Marx, Nietzsche, Darwin, Freud and the New Left. The triumph of pornography is both evidence of the death of God and one of the means by which he is killed.[17]

In other words, pornography is a "deathwork." Some sociological research shows there's a clear link between pornography use and the rejection of traditional religious belief particularly among teenagers.

The Therapeutic

Earlier in his opus, Trueman referred to the philosopher Alasdair MacIntyre and his book *After Virtue* which argues that modern moral theories are incapable of explaining the rational authority of moral norms. Into this void left by the failure of modern ethical theory has stepped what MacIntyre called "emotivism," in which all evaluative and moral judgments are "nothing but expressions of preference of attitude or feeling." This is similar to the Romantic poets. Trueman again: "Essentially emotivism presents preferences as if they were truth claims."[18] This is therapy culture in the courtroom. As we saw earlier, society's institutions must adapt to promote the psychological well-being of the individual. This has now entered the realm of the judiciary.

Commenting of the case of *Obergefell v. Hodges*—the case in which the Supreme Court legalized gay marriage—Trueman says

---

17 Trueman, 297

18 Trueman page 85

that the ethical logic used was mere emotivism consonant with the attitudes of sexualized therapeutic culture. He writes concerning the judgment:

> It is emotivism. Those parts of tradition that support contemporary tastes are proof positive of the correctness of the opinion; those that are not useful in supporting the desired conclusion or that stand in opposition to contemporary tastes can be dismissed as outmoded or motivated by bigotry or simply ignored. And the court can safely do this because it is speaking to a society at large that thinks precisely the same way. The ruling and its supporting arguments are absolutely connected to, and dependent on, the changes in thinking about selfhood, human nature, sexuality, and the nature of oppression and liberty that we have traced ... earlier.[19]

Transgenderism

Identity is now seen in terms of a self which is psychologized, sexual, and able to create and recreate itself. This paves the way for the idea of a person who sees themselves as being of one gender being trapped inside a body of another gender, or no longer wishing to be categorized as either male or female. Such ideas are coherent in a society which places a decisive priority on the psychological over the physical.

The LGBTQ+ coalition stands together against the traditional sexual norms of society. Transgender people make common cause with lesbians, gay men, and bisexual people because they perceive heterosexual normativity as the common enemy. However, the coalition doesn't easily fit together. There are contradictions. Both gay men and lesbians speak of themselves as *men* and *women* who are same-sex attracted. But that presupposes fixed genders. Those who argue for transgender and beyond don't accept the idea of fixed genders. They see gender as a fluid concept.

The status of transwomen (men who have become women) is a cause of acrimonious dispute among older feminists who campaigned for women's rights. The classic feminists feel that the whole status of being a woman is undermined and depoliticized by

---

19 Trueman page 315

transgenderism. Many feel that you cannot dissociate the female from female history and from the experience of what it is to grow up as a female physically. But, as Trueman notes, "being a woman is now something that can be produced by a technique—literally prescribed by a doctor."[20]

Transgenderism seems to repudiate the significance of the body for selfhood and this means a repudiation of parents—the ones who conceived, gave birth to, and raised the little girl or boy. Trueman quotes Germaine Greer: "Whatever else it is, gender reassignment is an exorcism of the mother."[21]

PART 4: WHAT TO THINK THROUGH

As we come to terms with this description of the sexual revolution and the world in which we now live, we ought to recognize that not everything going on is bad. There are two things in particular which Christians would do well to notice.

The *first* is dignity. Trueman writes, "With Rousseau's emphasis on the individual and the state of nature as the ideal, the shift to individual intrinsic dignity is clear. And that is something with which the Christian should sympathize. We are not supposed to regard the life of a poor person as of any less value than that of a wealthy or important public figure."[22] Unfortunately, this reclaimed dignity is detached from any sacred order. It's not rooted in all people being made in God's image (James 3:9).

The *second* is authenticity. Though Trueman doesn't say this, the concern of the sexual revolution for people to be outwardly what they are inwardly does find a positive echo in the New Testament—not in a sinful way but in a godly way. A great theme of Jesus' Sermon on the Mount is authenticity, the conviction that religious acts must come from the heart (Matthew 5:27–28; 6:1).

But generally speaking, Christians need to be extremely wary and discerning.

Engaging with LGBTQ+ Issues

Christians need to beware of simply taking on the world's way of thinking about these issues. Is the church meant to look "plausible"

20 Truemna page 360
21 Trueman page 375

22 Trueman, 387

to the world in its teaching about sexual ethics? Surely not. Our job is to love all people and remain faithful.

We can easily slip into using the categories of the world which are misleading. In doing so, we lose clarity on key issues. The idea that our true identity is sexual is wrong. The Genesis account tells us that sex is a *function* of who we are, not who we are (Genesis 1:27–28). Adam was a true human being before he ever had sex with Eve.

If the world's categories rest on a basic category mistake—that sexual desire is identity—then the Christian shouldn't simply allow themself to be defined within this LGBTQ+ framework. To concede the categories can concede the argument. Trueman writes, "The framework for identity in wider society is deep rooted, powerful and fundamentally antithetical to the kind of identity promoted as basic in the Bible."[23]

Sexual Morality

The sexual revolution has been built on the idea that sex is meant to simply be recreational fun. Unfortunately, the consequences of

"free love" have been largely avoided through abortion and medicine. But deep difficulties have begun to emerge.

First, the "free love" approach, as Freud foresaw, favors the powerful. The #MeToo movement has rightly exposed this. The world recognizes the horror of these things.

Second, under the sexual revolution, sex is meant to be fine between "consenting adults." But as many court cases have found, defining consent is very difficult. What one partner took to be consent was not meant as such by the other partner. Even on its own terms, this cries out for setting sex within a moral framework. But of course, this is the last thing the sexual revolution wants to do.

Gay Marriage

In *After the Ball: How America Will Conquer Its Fear and Hatred of Gays,* neuropsychologist Marshall Kirk and advertising executive Hunter Madse advised the gay community that if it wanted to gain acceptance it needed to project a more cute and cuddly image of itself. Gay marriage has now arrived and has all the therapeutic rhetoric and images on its side. It seems as

---

23 Trueman, 393

if it's here to stay, so faithful Christians will need to think through how to cope and address this fact.

It may be that its weakness will be the way that marriage has had to be redefined in order to make room for it. Perhaps the door has been opened by the legislation to other forms of "marriage" which will not prove so appealing to the Western public. For example, does it make polygamous arrangements possible, which may well lead to the misuse and abuse of women?

When we mix same-sex marriage with transgenderism, more problems arise. Trueman tells the story of a lesbian marriage in which one of the women became a man. The partner was left in total confusion. She didn't know who she was. Was she a "straight" wife married to a man? But if she was a lesbian, then why was she married to a man?

Religious Freedom

In paragraph 18 of its Universal Declaration of Human Rights, the United Nations guarantees freedom of religion and freedom to change religion. But the expressive individualism of the sexual revolution is putting pressure on religious freedom.

The general decline in religious commitment in the West, and especially the loss of younger people, means that society doesn't care very much about religious freedom. Religious people and Christians are vulnerable to having their freedoms curtailed and perhaps even eventually removed. In the West, it's presently thought that sexual desire is the key to personal identity and therefore the dignity of every individual. This trumps religious freedom, which means that society sees the church as something it would probably be better off without.

PART 5: HOW CHURCHES SHOULD RESPOND

How should churches respond? Some conservative evangelicals have simply continued their same old path hoping that the things we've discussed will simply go away or pass them by. That's unlikely. Other churches have compromised on the Bible's clear teaching on sexual ethics or at least tried to create some "wiggle room."

Every pastor needs to open his Bible with humility. He needs to pray for wisdom about how to lead the church at this time. Here are three suggestions.

Biblical Identity

Surely one of the first things that conservative evangelical churches ought to be doing is clearly teaching human identity. Among other things, this will include teaching on the image of God, what it means to be fallen, and what it means to be redeemed. We need to teach a biblical understanding of the physical body, which will be just as important as a biblical understanding of work, art, sexuality, ethnicity, justice, etc.[24]

Explicitly, when a young man comes to his pastor and says, "I think I'm gay" or a girl privately confesses to her mother, "I think I might be a lesbian" the first response needs to be something like lovingly saying, "But you are so much more than your current sexual temptations." The contemporary world narrows people down to their hormones. But human beings are gloriously so much bigger than mere sex machines. The whole history of mankind's achievements in science, art, and humanitarianism shouts this

from the rooftops. We are "God's offspring" (Acts 17:28). So pastor, our sermons must help people break away from the ugly solitary confinement of trivialized sensual humanity. Humanity is being trashed, and we are called to rescue it.

Right and Wrong

When people are "lovers of themselves," then what's good tends to be seen as what "feels good," and what's bad is simply what makes us "feel bad." The church easily gets sucked into this way of thinking because making people immediately feel better seems so loving.

But even common sense tells us that this is too simplistic. Chemotherapy doesn't make a sufferer feel good, but terribly bad, at least to begin. In spiritual terms, conviction of sin isn't a nice feeling, but it does lead us to see our need of Christ and his cross (Acts 2:37). Trueman writes:

> The church should reflect long and hard on the connection between aesthetics and her core beliefs and practices. I noted above that one of the hallmarks of ethical discussion today is its

---

24 See for example *Re-enchanting Humanity: a theology of mankind* by Owen Strachan, Mentor Christian Focus, 2019

dependence on personal narratives. ... Personal narratives (are) presented as incontrovertible precisely because they are personal testimonies—the highest form of authority in an age of expressive individualism. And this aesthetic concern reflects the perennial power of sympathy and empathy in shaping morality. ... The church needs to respond to this aesthetic-based logic, but first of all she needs to be consciously aware of it. And that means that she herself must forgo indulging in, and thereby legitimating, the kind of aesthetic strategy in the wider culture. The debate on LGBTQ+ issues within the church must be decided on the basis of moral principles, not the attractiveness and appeal of the narratives involved. ... That is not to say that pastoral strategies aimed at individuals should not be compassionate, but what is and what is not compassionate must always rest on deeper, transcendent principles.[25]

---

25 Trueman, pages 402-403

Put simply, churches need to come back to the Bible. Christianity must be properly doctrinal and dogmatic.

Church as Family

Human selfhood depends on community. Our identity is at least partially constructed by our social interactions.

This means that if churches want to help people find and maintain their true identity, then they must be communities that mirror and build the image of God in people. A church shouldn't be cultish. It should be a home for true humanity. It should be a family. And there should be a deep humility, recognizing that every saint has a past and every sinner has a future, under Christ's kingship.

Churches that have chosen to operate as corporations or educational institutions really miss the point. The phrase "brothers and sisters" really means something. As the world misleads people about their true identity, the church will become increasingly crucial.

ABOUT THE AUTHOR
John Benton is the Director for Pastoral Support for the Pastors' Academy at London Seminary.

Book Review: Carl Trueman's *Strange New World*

HOW DID WE GET HERE?

Allen Duty

The world has changed. Things are not the way they were 60 years ago, 30 years ago, or even 10 years ago, especially in America. These changes feel drastic and sudden, like a revolution fought and won overnight.

While many in our society celebrate these changes, many others—particularly Christians—lament. We find ourselves wondering:

- How was gay marriage legalized less than 20 years after a democratic president signed the Defense of Marriage Act into law?
- How can we allow men who identify as women to compete against (and usually defeat) biological females less than 50 years after Title IX was signed into law?
- How is it that a book questioning the transgender narrative was banned from Amazon when Mein Kampf is still for sale?
- How? How did we get here?

These are the questions that Carl R. Trueman is seeking to answer in *Strange New World: How Thinkers an Activists Redefined Identity and Sparked the Sexual Revolution.*

Trueman's earlier work, *The Rise and Triumph of the Modern Self: Cultural Amnesia, Expressive Individualism, and the Road to Sexual Revolution*, is by all accounts a masterful treatment of the subject. But it's a seven-course meal: 400 pages of detailed history and thorough argumentation. That seemed too much to stomach for many potential readers, so Trueman wrote this volume to present his thesis in a more digestible size.

THE LONG, WINDING ROAD TO REVOLUTION

Many Christians look back to the sexual revolution of the 1960s and conclude that most, if not all, of our current problems began there. But Trueman shows that the road to the sexual revolution was paved hundreds of years earlier by the advent and increasing influence of a worldview that American scholar Robert Bellah coined "expressive individualism." This worldview demands that our inner feelings must be expressed if we are to become our true selves.

Trueman offers a convincing argument that this worldview began with Romantic thinkers Descartes and Rousseau, who granted final authority to inner feelings, which are always pure and true guides to who human beings are.

Marx and Nietzsche then politicized these beliefs. Marx argued that morality is historically conditioned and designed to maintain unjust structures, and Neitzsche argued that morality is a fiction invented by one group to subordinate another. For both men, moral codes are manipulative and must be transgressed if true freedom is to be found.

Finally, Freud and Reich sexualized the psychology that Marx and Nietzsche politicized. Freud argued that sex is foundational to human identity and happiness. In his mind, sex isn't something we do; it is who we are. The labels "straight," "gay," and "bisexual" make sense even when applied to people who have never engaged in sexual activity. Reich argued that because sex is foundational to human happiness and inextricably linked with our identity, the State must take a proactive stance in promoting sexual freedom.

Trueman shows that by the time of the sexual revolution of the 1960s, the hippies weren't blazing a new trail. They were walking down a completed road that had been in construction for several hundred years.

That road leads directly to our current destination—a world where only hours after his inauguration, our president signed into law an executive order requiring public buildings to open women's restrooms to biological men identifying as women. That's only possible in a world that believes our feelings are the true and infallible guide to who we really are; that sex is foundational to human identity and happiness; and that the State must therefore protect and promote sexual freedom.

YOU CAN RUN, BUT YOU CAN'T HIDE FOREVER

If you don't live in an urban context or a university town, it's possible that your daily life has been largely unaffected by the aggressive activism of those who support the transgender narrative. But as they say, it's coming soon to a theater near you—and that theater is your local government, your child's elementary school, and even your own workplace.

Since the rise of the Moral Majority in the 1980s, many Christian and conservative leaders have declared war on the culture, believing that the only way to win it back is through activism and political engagement, which usually means political victory for the "right" candidates.

Trueman respectfully disagrees with that approach. He writes, "I am not here calling for a kind of passive quietism whereby Christians abdicate their civic responsibilities or make no connection between how to pursue those civic responsibilities and their religious beliefs. I am suggesting rather that engaging in cultural warfare using the world's tools, rhetoric, and weapons *is not the way for God's people*" (177, italics mine).

Instead, he advocates an approach that is biblically rooted and confident in the sovereignty of God to achieve his purposes through his people. He counsels readers to begin with self-examination, repenting for the ways we have compromised the gospel by conforming to the spirit of this age.

He encourages us to humbly recognize where we have been complicit in lending credibility to expressive individualism, from the way we approach the church as consumers looking to have our felt needs met, to the way our worship music tends to use individual pronouns and overemphasize feelings, to the way we've accepted no-fault divorce on the grounds that personal happiness has not been met.

Finally, and most importantly, Trueman argues that the best way to engage the culture is to protest it by offering a true vision of what it means to be a human being made in the image of God. Since modern sexual and identity politics are functions of deeper notions of selfhood, we must understand the Christian view of the self; and since the self is created in God's image, we must hold a biblical doctrine of God.

Identity is shaped by the communities to which we belong, so the church must be our strongest community, and we must invite others to come, see, and experience that supernatural community, which Jesus said would persuade others that we are truly his disciples (John 13:35).

THE BUILDING IS COMING DOWN—ARE YOU READY?

Strange New World is a remarkable combination of depth and readability, clearly presenting the arguments from his earlier work without sacrificing essential background information or insightful analysis.

Each chapter concludes with questions that are well-suited for individual reflection or group study. And though it may sound bleak, ultimately, the book is hopeful, arguing that Christians in this strange new world shouldn't despair, but rather should work to prepare themselves for the task at hand, keeping God's unbreakable promises before our eyes.

The worldview of expressive individualism is built on the idea that authenticity is achieved by acting outwardly in accordance with our feelings. This ideological structure is destined to collapse.

When it does, Christians must be the first responders, running to the rubble to remove those who have been seriously wounded, and to apply the healing balm of the gospel.

Trueman's work will help train you for that upcoming mission.

ABOUT THE AUTHOR

Allen Duty is the preaching pastor at New Life Baptist Church in College Station, Texas. You can find him on Twitter at @AllenDuty.

How Do We Find Our Identity in Christ?

AN EXCERPT FROM BRIAN ROSNER'S *HOW TO FIND YOURSELF*

As odd as it sounds, the narrative identity of believers in Christ is tied up with the life story of Jesus Christ, which itself echoes the experience of God's people in the Old Testament.

With respect to the question of personal identity, if we wonder who we are, Jesus Christ is the one and only perfect human being. In one sense, there are only two basic identities in the world. In the book of Genesis, Adam, the first human being, is the prototype of us all, created in God's image but flawed and marred by sin. Jesus Christ is the second Adam, the one who gets it right, and the prototype and forerunner of all who put their trust in him.

With Jesus, we see what new humanity looks like. As Oliver O'Donovan puts it, "The new man Christ is the pattern to which we may conform ourselves."[26] But it's not just a matter of imitating him. In the Gospels, there is a call to follow Jesus literally. But the New Testament letters, written after Jesus rose from the dead and ascended to heaven, never talk about following Jesus. "Following" is inadequate language to describe Christ's impact on our identity. The apostles prefer to describe people as being "in Christ" rather than following him.

---

26 Oliver O'Donovan, *Resurrection and Moral Order: An Outline for Evangelical Ethics* (Leicester: Apollos, 1994), 143.

The language of being "in Christ" is among the most puzzling in the New Testament. While it can mean that we belong to Christ, on occasions it means something more. Paul can use the notion of being "in Christ" to indicate that we actually participate in Christ's very identity: "if anyone is in Christ, he is a new creation" (2 Cor. 5:17). And the goal of Paul's pastoral ministry is to "present everyone mature in Christ" (Col. 1:28).

Andrew Cameron has explored the idea of finding your identity "in Christ":

Whoever we think ourselves to be, Jesus' humanity encompasses and "decodes" everyone's diversity, all journeys, and every vocation. To be truly human involves knowing him and participating with him. Somehow, to participate "in Christ" is to begin a new voyage of discovery. We do not lose our past stories, yet we increasingly understand our selves in reference to Jesus Christ.[27]

The new self we are to put on is Jesus Christ, who represents God's new humanity. It is not that we thereby lose our individuality. But who we are is brought to completion in him.

The defining moment of the lives of those living the life story of Jesus Christ is his death on a cross. The direction of our lives is set by that defining moment. Living authentically, then, becomes the task of living in accordance with your new identity and regularly performing your signature move. According to Colossians 3, we died and rose to new life in union with Christ (3:1–4). That is our "moment of truth," the memory of which defines us forever. It changes everything for us. And we would not be who we are were it not for Christ's death and resurrection.

And the signature move that grows out of that identity is the act of love. Our conduct is to be compassionate, kind, humble, gentle, patient, and forgiving, all of which grow out of "love, which binds everything together in perfect harmony" (3:14). Just as our identity as children of God was forged through an act of amazing love,

27 Andrew Cameron, *Joined-up life: A Christian Account of How Ethics Works* (Nottingham, England: IVP, 2011), 114.

so too we are to live lives of costly, selfless, others-centered love.

It is not that other identity markers and what you do with your life are of no consequence for your personal identity if you are a believer in Christ. Your race, gender, family, occupation, marital status, and so on are important, but they are not all-important.

Obviously, life events and experiences can have a lasting impact on your identity and conduct. But at the most profound level, if you are a believer in Jesus Christ, what sets the course for your life and keeps it on track is your identification with Christ and imitation of him and being known and loved by God as his child. Putting on that identity will determine the sort of man or woman, worker, friend, neighbor, father or mother, son or daughter that you will become.

EDITOR'S NOTE

Content taken from *How to Find Yourself* by Brian Rosner, ©2022. Used by permission of Crossway, a publishing ministry of Good News Publishers.

Expressive Individualism and the Church

Carl Trueman

There is a real danger for Christians as they assess many modern developments regarding the human person—whether matters of sex and sexuality, abortion, euthanasia, or simply what we might call the generally self-centered nature of modern consumerist life. That danger is the one committed by the Pharisee in the Temple, the one who uttered the words, "I thank you, Lord, that I am not like other men." That prayer immediately set him apart from his contemporaries and exempted him, at least in his own eyes, from the moral problems of his age.

EXPRESSIVE INDIVIDUALISM IN CONTEMPORARY WORSHIP

If expressive individualism is the typical way in which people think of themselves and their relationship to the world, then Christians must understand that they too are deeply implicated. We can no more abstract ourselves from our social and cultural context, and the intuitions that our context cultivates, than we can leave our bodies and float to the moon. Indeed, our first thought must not be that of the Pharisee but rather that of the disciples when Jesus told them that *one of them* would betray him, "Is it I, Lord?" Such an approach will not only reflect and reinforce appropriate humility; it may also help to free us just a little from the culture that surrounds us. To know how the world encourages us to think and live will equip us to resist it.

Simply put, expressive individualism pervades modern Christian life. Those of us who attend churches with a traditionalist worship aesthetic would likely point to modern praise songs and worship styles as evidence for this. Many Christians view worship as a time to "express themselves"; in doing so, they highlight the benefits of "spontaneity," or musical arrangements that play to the emotions, or lyrics that focus on first-person-singular feelings. This is low-hanging fruit to make the case that modern Christianity is deeply shaped by expressive individualism.

While the expression of feelings in worship is certainly not wrong—the Psalms are replete with such—the focus on emotions too often becomes an end in itself rather than a stage on the road to bringing those feelings into conformity with God's Word. The inner psychological state of the psalmist is always ultimately to be interpreted through the grid of God's revelation. Even Psalm 88, the bleakest psalm with the most painful expressions of desolation, addresses God at the start by his covenant name. The despair is still to be set within the context of God's covenant commitment to his people. In the world of expressive individualism, however, the truth of emotions is found not in their conformity to God's revelation but in the sincerity of their expression. When that characterizes a worship song, whether in terms of lyrics or music, it is highly problematic.

So there are legitimate grounds for seeing expressive individualism in contemporary worship.

But the situation is more subtle than that, and worship traditionalists do not have legitimate cause to reach for the words of the pharisee's prayer simply because they are traditionalists. If one of the central elements of expressive individualism is the notion that the individual makes choices about life based upon personal preference, there is no reason why the traditionalist choice of, say, The Book of Common Prayer liturgy over modern praise songs is in itself irrefutable evidence that expressive individualism is not at work. The words may be superior and more theologically substantial but that does not mean that my choice is not driven primarily by personal aesthetic preference rather than truly objective value.

Here's the key question to ask: "Why do we worship?" Not "we" as in some abstracted notion of the people of God but "we" as individuals. Do we worship to be made to feel good or do we worship as a response to the being and work of a holy God, and thereby conform ourselves (and understand our experiences and feelings) in light of that God? Unless it is the latter then we are allowing our own complicity in expressive individualism to drive our worship.

EXPRESSIVE INDIVIDUALISM AND CHURCH COMMITMENT

But expressive individualism affects more than just worship. It also shapes how we think of church commitment. This problem is even trickier to parse. Freedom of religion is a social good. Who of us wants to live in a country where we would face prosecution and perhaps imprisonment for practicing our Christian faith? Yet here is the rub: when a country enjoys religious freedom, power tilts toward the congregant and individual churches become competitors in the religious marketplace. Unlike the Middle Ages in Europe, or even the Reformation world before travel over distances became swift and easy, today's Christian cannot avoid having to choose a church. After all, there's almost always more than one option. We may not all use the obnoxious phrase "church shopping," but none of us can actually avoid doing it. Freedom of religion, rather like democracy itself, is not an unmitigated virtue, albeit preferable to any of the other options.

And this applies not simply to the initial choice of congregation but to continued commitment to that congregation. Membership vows ought to be solemn and serious. And yet how many are routinely broken as people move from one church to the next for the most trivial of reasons? Again, this is expressive individualism, manifesting itself as a form of religious consumerism. If there's something I don't like in church—maybe it's the pastor's choice of tie (or his lack of tie), maybe it's the hymnbook or the order of worship, or maybe it's just the fact that the initial buzz of being a new member has faded away—I can move on to somewhere else that suits my tastes better.

This perhaps finds its most dramatic outworking in church government and discipleship. The expressive individual is the sovereign individual. All other relationships—to other people, to institutions, to those who hold office in such institutions—is subordinate to the personal needs and feelings of me as an individual. Thus, I can choose whether to acknowledge their authority. I can choose what my commitment to them should involve, and how I should treat any counsel they give me. I decide how I should respond to any attempt to rebuke or discipline me. I am the sovereign arbiter of what is good for me. Everybody else can practically give me nothing more than pious advice based upon their opinion.

HOW CAN WE ESCAPE?

Given that expressive individualism defines our cultural atmosphere at this time, and that we Christians are no more exempt than anyone else, there's perhaps a temptation here to despair. How can we escape from that which we cannot escape? Like our sinful natures, expressive individualism is something that will inform our intuitions and our understanding until the day we die. Yet as with our sinful natures, there are things we can do.

First, simply being aware of the reality of our situation is important, for that allows us to engage in self-examination. Second, we should consciously reflect upon our real motives for some of our most intuitive beliefs and behavior. For example, why do we go to the church we go to? Why do we enjoy its worship? Of course, such reflection must be shaped by what Martin Luther called "the Word that comes from outside," that is, the regular preaching of God's Word which, as applied by the Spirit, makes such self-examination possible. And finally, we must repent of our expressive individualism not just in general but in those specific areas that the Spirit brings to our attention.

Is this a perfect approach? Far from it. As with all areas of sanctification, it is one that will never be perfected in this life. But that does not mean there cannot be Spirit-empowered growth. And that is what we must pray for.

ABOUT THE AUTHOR

Carl Trueman is a Professor of Biblical and Religious Studies at Grove City College in Grove City, Pennsylvania.

Preaching in the Age of Expressive Individualism

TELLING THE STORY OF OUR NEW IDENTITY

Michael Lawrence

A few weeks ago, in a Sunday school class discussion, an older member of my church described evangelism as "sharing my truth." I was taken aback when I heard it, as this was no Millennial or Gen Z "woke" culture warrior, but an older Boomer. It's quite possible they didn't understand what the phrase meant in modern parlance, but it brought home to me how far our culture has moved when it did not even register to this dear older saint that the significance of the gospel is found precisely in the fact that it is not "my truth," but "the truth."

Like it or not, we're all swimming in the cultural waters of expressive individualism. This is more than simply radical moral relativism. It's the rejection of essential human nature for untethered subjective sentiment. It's the replacement of ethics with personal preference and the meaning of life with the self-creation of identity. Its most extreme expressions are seen in transgenderism and modern identity politics, but its impact is far more subtle and insidious, as the opening example shows. If even our older, more mature church members are affected by the habits of thought of expressive individualism, what's a pastor to do?

Preach the Word.

In our weekly sermons, expositing God's Word for God's people, we have been given everything we need to make disciples in the age of expressive individualism. I want to highlight two points of application in our preaching that can help combat the corrosive and corrupting influence of the spirit of our age.

IDENTITY R US

While the emphasis on our identity in Christ in modern evangelicalism is relatively recent, there's no question that Scripture has much to say on the topic. From Israel's call to be distinct and holy among the nations (Ex. 19:6), to Paul's emphasis on the new creation (2 Cor. 5:17), to Jesus' declaration, "You are the light of the world," (Matt. 5:14), the Scriptures are replete with language that defines who we are, both individually and corporately. And in this language, we have an opportunity to push back against the foundation of expressive individualism, and not just its outworking.

So often in our sermon application, we tend to focus on moral imperatives or ethical implications. So, for example, in a few weeks I'll be preaching from Esther 1. It would be very easy for me to exclusively focus my application on the ethical imperative of godly submission to authority in the home and the state. And I wouldn't be wrong to do so. But in the context of this cultural moment, many in our congregations will intuitively feel that such authority is arbitrary, and maybe even oppressive. If I'm going to apply my text effectively, I'll need to take a step back from the ethical imperative and address the foundational question of human and Christian identity that gives the imperative moral force. That might mean addressing our identity as gendered beings. That might mean addressing our identity as image bearers of God, created to both exercise and submit to authority. It will certainly mean explaining that our submission to human authority is always, "as to the Lord" (Col 3:18). Therefore, far from a demeaning experience of subjugation, respect for authority is an act of worship that flows from our identity as servants of the King of Kings and Lord of Lords.

Never miss an opportunity in whatever text you're in to define your people's identity according to the Scriptures. What does it mean to be a man or woman? What does it mean to be a Christian? What does it mean to be the body and bride of Christ? Don't simply tell your people what to do. Remind them who they are, by dint of creation and new creation, because identity, not behavior, is where the battle is being fought, and either won or lost.

STORY-TIME

If you ask me who I am, I'll tell you a story: I'm the adopted, first-born son of a prosperous southern family whose world got turned upside down when I met the Lord in college. I'm the husband of a beautiful New England Yankee and the father of five who won't be an empty nester until close to retirement. I'm the pastor of a west coast church who doesn't have any family east of the Appalachians. Those

look like three propositional statements, but if you look closely, each of them tells a story, and those stories define who I am.

We make sense of our lives through narratives. Expressive individualism is no different. Building on the base of consumerism, "I am what I own," and modern psychology, "I am what I desire," expressive individualism defines the individual through the heroic arc of self-creation against the oppressive forces of bigotry, conventional morality, and even biology. It's an intoxicating story, but hardly a new one.

It began in the garden of Eden, when Satan lied to the woman and said, "In fact, God knows that when you eat it your eyes will be opened, and you will be like God" (Gen 3:5). It continued at Babel, when humanity determined to "make a name for ourselves" (Gen 11:4) through their grandiose building plans. And it continues today.

We have a better story. It's the story of God's creation of this world, our place in it, its fall into corruption, and his determination to rescue us from it and bring us to a better place through the life, death, resurrection, and second coming of his Son. It's a better story because it's true. But it's also a better story because of its power to explain our present experience and its ability to provide us a future hope.

We often think of Scripture as an ancient book we look back upon, to mine for insight, instruction, or inspiration. But that's to misunderstand what we're dealing with. The Bible is telling the grand story of creation, fall, redemption, and consummation. It begins at the beginning and ends at the end. And since we're not at the end yet, it's a story that contains us. We don't look back it. We're caught up in it. And therefore, the story of Scripture is our story, the story that defines who we are, where we came from, and where we're going. If we're going to push back against the false narrative of expressive individualism, we need to do more than simply show the absurdity of heroic self-creation. We must help people see themselves inside the identity-forming narrative that is the history of redemption.

To return to Esther 1, it would be easy to give my congregation a history lesson on the Persian empire. But what they need to see is that God's providential rule over an ancient Persian king in order to rescue his people from destruction was a picture and foreshadowing of his providential rule over both a Roman ruler and Satan himself in order to deliver his Son to the cross and so deliver his people from death and hell forever. And therefore, they can be certain that whatever the kingdoms and cultures of this world bring against them, "the kingdom of the world [will] become the kingdom of our Lord and of his Christ and he will reign forever and ever." (Rev. 11:15) The strength to persevere in faith against the allurements of expressive individualism does not come simply from the hope of heaven, but from the confidence that what God has done in the past he will do again in the future.

ONE LITTLE WORD

For hundreds of years in the West, we have had the blessing of a culture that in many ways reinforced and even affirmed our message. Those days are increasingly behind us. Our culture, which has for so long drawn on its Christian heritage even while denying it, is now finding that account empty, even overdrawn. I don't think it's an overstatement to say that our culture is (re)turning to paganism. And there's no reason to think that such a turn can be reversed.

But that doesn't mean that our task has changed. Ours were never the culture wars to begin with. Our fight is not against flesh and blood, but "against the cosmic powers of this darkness" (Eph. 6:12). And for that battle, our weapons have not changed. As Martin Luther penned long ago, "the prince of darkness grim, we tremble not for him. His rage we can endure, for lo, his doom is sure. One little word shall fell him."

Preach the word. Apply it to your people's lives. Tell them who they are in Christ. Remind them where they are in his story. The Word will do the rest.

ABOUT THE AUTHOR
Michael Lawrence is the senior pastor of Hinson Baptist Church in Portland, Oregon. You can find him on Twitter at @pdxtml.

Pastoring Singles in the Age of Self

Sam Allberry

When the French philosopher Rene Descartes famously declared "I think therefore I am" he was (among other things) establishing a trend that has reached full fruition in our own day: starting the answer to life's biggest questions with "I." We find ourselves now living in the "Age of Self."[28] If the basic unit of life is "me," then the fundamental goal of life is my own sense of fulfilment, not least sexually.

Such a context makes the Christian life of singleness all the more challenging, and the healthy pastoring of single people all the more urgent. Every generation has faced the pressure to regard the Christian sexual ethic as unnecessarily restrictive. But today we face the formidable cultural pressure to see that ethic as dangerous to our psychological health and an existential threat to societal good. Without careful shepherding, many of our singles will get caught in the riptides of these social currents and carried far away from Christ.

---

28 See Carl R. Trueman's landmark work *The Rise and Triumph of the Modern Self: Cultural Amnesia, Expressive Individualism, and the Road to the Sexual Revolution* (Wheaton, Illinois: Crossway, 2020) for more on this. A condensed and more accessible version is Carl R. Trueman, *Strange New World: How Thinkers and Activists Redefined Identity and Sparked the Sexual Revolution* (Wheaton, Illinois: Crossway, 2022).

So how can we pastor singles in such a time? There are three truths in which we especially need to immerse the church, and especially our singles.

1. MARITAL STATUS IS NOT THE PRIMARY DETERMINER OF FULFILMENT AND HAPPINESS.

It is easy to think it is. Culturally, the message we hear on constant repeat is that a life without a significant romantic other is barely a life at all--certainly not one that can be full. A friend of mine watched three movies in a row on a long-haul flight, one a comedy, one a superhero movie, and one a more serious movie. He said each of them reflected this same message: you are a profound loser if you're not romantically fulfilled.

Sometimes the message in the church is not that different. We might put marriage in the place of romantic fulfilment but attach the very same significance to it. Much of church life is structured around married couples and families that it can be hard to know how to fit in as a single person. We can often speak of marriage as if it is the telos of the

Christian life, something we graduate out of singleness into.

So it's understandable if many in our churches feel as though the opportunity to get married is going to be the single most significant determiner of whether they can basically be happy in life. The messaging all around us seems to reinforce this.

But the Bible show us a very different way of thinking. It is not the binary of single/married that will most profoundly determine our potential future happiness; it is the binary of being in Christ or not. Paul's repeated message to his Philippian friends was not "rejoice in marriage always," or even "rejoice in romantic fulfilment," but "rejoice in the Lord always" (Phil. 4:4). He is where our deepest joy and fulfilment are to be found. When we find our ultimate contentment in Christ, we realize it doesn't ultimately matter if we are married or single. We will not be missing out on the best life has to offer if we have Christ.

Pastoral experience bears this out. Even the best marriages will disappoint us at times. I've met and pastored many people who thought getting married would fill the deepest longings in life, only to discover it can even expand those longings. A life in Jesus, not a ring on a finger, is the only thing that can truly satisfy.

2. MARRIAGE AND SINGLENESS ARE NOT ABOUT US.

In 1 Cor. 7:7, Paul describes both marriage and singleness as gifts of God. They both come to us as good gifts from our generous Creator. Neither is to be demeaned or disparaged. Each is to be received with thankfulness. And like all of God's good gifts, it is to be stewarded well. Like the spiritual gifts Paul goes on to speak of later in the same letter, marriage and singleness are not ends in themselves; they are for "the common good" (1 Cor. 12:7).

So the end-point of singleness—and marriage, for that matter—is not my own sense of fulfilment or satisfaction. It is easy to practice "selfish singleness"—to take the freedoms and opportunities of singleness purely as a way of serving our own happiness. We can take the lack of marital commitment or parental responsibility simply as a means to do what we want. But this is not to follow God's design for us. If what attracts us is the lack of other people to be constrained by, then we have missed not only the point of singleness, but the point of the Christian life.

Paul's positivity about singleness––often surprising to our contemporary ears—focuses on the opportunities it presents for service, not for self-fulfilment. In place of the constraints of family is to be "undivided devotion to the Lord" (1 Cor. 7:35). This is such a desirable outcome to Paul that he could "wish that all were as I myself am"—single. So what should motivate singles about possibly remaining single is not delaying commitment, or having more disposable income, but the freedom to serve the Lord in ways that might not be possible or advisable if one were married.

3. GODLY SINGLENESS IS JUST WHAT WE NEED IN THE AGE OF SELF.

As we come to terms with the Age of Self in which we find ourselves, we might realise that many of these opportunities singles have for "undivided devotion" to Christ and his cause are precisely what we need in such a time as this.

Take just one example: the Age of Self is desperately lacking in community. Singles are not the only ones who have something to contribute on this front, but there is a unique way in which singleness can be used to lubricate community within our churches. Many singles have a greater capacity for friendship than married people. Simply put, it is possible to "fit more people in." That greater capacity can enable singles to meaningfully befriend a wider spectrum of people—to form deep friendships across generations and other groupings. Singles might have more opportunity than others to move between and be a means of connecting varying demographics, connecting people that might otherwise have little occasion to encounter one another. Singles can be great at introducing disparate people. Singles can be uniquely instrumental in helping to foster the very forms of thick and diverse community we need in this cultural moment, singles.

Or consider the ways godly singleness can be an answer to the deep confusion many experience when it comes to issues of identity and sexuality. So much is freighted on being romantically or sexually fulfilled: it has come to be one of the greatest goods in contemporary western society. Now consider the Christian single who finds their deepest longings met in Christ and lives in glad service of others. Such people are a prophetic counterpoint to the world around us. Life is not about me. Sex is not about me. There is one who is a bridegroom—one so complete in all his perfections that he can eclipse even the most intense romantic experiences this world has to offer. One whose future life with his people is so complete and full that we will not need to be married or given in marriage in the age to come (Matt. 22:30).

The Age of Self is likely to be with us for some time. But the answer to all the seemingly unassailable "Ages" of this world is the gospel of that single man, Jesus Christ, whose Word will always lead us in good paths, and whose life with us is sufficient for all our greatest needs and longings.

ABOUT THE AUTHOR

Sam Allberry is one of the pastors at St Mary's Anglican Church, Maidenhead, UK. He is also an author of the book Is God Anti-Gay?

Youth Ministry and the Rise and Triumph of the Modern Self

Walt Mueller

Perhaps you've seen it on TV or heard it on the radio. An ad begins with a host of happy and energetic young voices talking on top of each other. Then, a narrator asks the question: "What do *you* want to be?" After several responses from teens regarding their confusing quest to establish their identity, we hear the invitation: "Whoever you want to be, it's yours to make on Instagram!"

Two thoughts jumped into my head. First, Instagram's marketing team has really tapped into our kids' urgent yearning to answer that all-important question: "Who am I?" Of course, it's hard to imagine a more dangerous guide than Instagram. Which leads me to my second thought, one that's short and sweet: "Ugghh!"

Because we all swim in the so-called cultural soup, it's easy to miss the significance of this 30-second Instagram ad. But if we take the time to reflect on this cultural artifact, it's clear that it's both *directive* and *reflective*.

As a *directive* piece, it lays out a map for our vulnerable kids to follow in order to find their way on the identity-formation trail. As a *reflective* piece, it offers us a wide-open look into the basic beliefs we embrace about who we are as humans.

In his book, *The Rise and Triumph of the Modern Self: Cultural Amnesia, Expressive Individualism, and the Road to the Sexual Revolution,* Carl Trueman lifts readers out of the cultural soup to help us understand the magnitude of the changes taking place. His explanatory journey through the history of ideas that led us to "expressive individualism" is brilliant. Our kids most likely can't consciously name or explain expressive individualism, but they've unconsciously assimilated it into just about every fabric of their lives, most obviously in their progressive views on sexuality and gender.

In this article, I want to ask a few questions: "Have our youth ministries been complicit in expressive individualism's cancerous spread within the body of Christ? If so, how has the rise and triumph of the modern self subtly triumphed over and reshaped both the content of our teaching and our ministry forms and practices?

As I read *The Rise and Triumph of the Modern Self,* I couldn't help but think about how our ministry efforts should endeavor to *form* kids into the identity for which they've been created, rather than allowing them to embrace a *de-formed* identity of their own emotionally-driven creation. Our youth ministries should foster a lifestyle of faithfully following Jesus while denying oneself (Mark 8:34–37) by emphasizing biblical truth through thoughtful ministry practices.

THE WHAT—BIBLICAL TRUTH

From the day they were born, our kids have grown up in a world that scoffs at submission to any authority outside of oneself. The sovereignty of God and the authority of Scripture are outdated remnants. After all, sovereignty and authority reside in the self. So intuition drives beliefs and behaviors as we encourage each other to find and express "*my* truth."

When kids are nurtured from birth into thinking "it's all about you," "follow your heart," and "you do you," it should come as no surprise that we now have a generation of young people who are increasingly de-coupled from and ignorant of authoritative truth-claims about God and the universe in general and orthodox Christianity in particular. As Tara Isabella Burton wrote in her 2020 book *Strange Rites: New Religions for a Godless World*, we have "a religion of emotive intuition, of aestheticized and commodified experience, of self-creation and self-improvement, and yes, selfies."

But not only do you make yourself, you also make your own god(s). Consider the concluding pages of the recent children's book, *What Is God Like?*, by Rachel Held Evans and Matthew Paul Turner. "What is God like? That's a very big question, one that people from places all around the world, throughout all time, have answered in many different ways. Keep searching. Keep wondering. Keep learning about God. But whenever you aren't sure what God is like, think about what

makes you feel safe, what makes you feel brave, and what makes you feel loved." As one discerning mom said to me after reading the book, "My security system makes me feel safe, warm chocolate chip cookies make me feel loved, and a couple glasses of wine make me feel brave. Not sure that's a great description of God, though."

While we would all agree (I hope!) that we must diligently nurture our kids in all the authoritative truths of God's Word, let me suggest four topics that come to mind as increasingly necessary in light of the cultural narrative shaping our kids. For youth pastors, I suggest you stake these truths into the ground, mentioning them as often as you can.

FIRST, WE MUST TEACH A BIBLICAL THEOLOGY OF IDENTITY.

Carl Trueman describes our world as a place where "human beings are called to transcend themselves, to make their lives into works of art, to take the place of God as self-creators and inventors, not discoverers of meaning" (42). Our kids are answering the question

"Who am I?" in a world that idolizes the immanent and looks down on the transcendent, a world in which our identities are created, even curated, for public consumption and affirmation. Of course, even our most well-intentioned attempts at creating our own identity are doomed to fail, which is why identical these days are often considered "fluid." . Think the gender and sexuality spectrums. We choose and choose and choose again, morphing and changing in search of the satisfaction. Os Guinness states it well, "People are always becoming, but they never become anything for long."

To dissuade young people from believing these lies, current youth ministries must point and keep pointing to the Creation narratives. This is where we discover that God has already fastened an identity to us: we are image-bearers infused with value, dignity, and worth.

By teaching the Creation narratives, we'll also find God's order and design for sexuality and gender. So as we see kids transformed and saved by the grace of God through Jesus Christ, we must nurture them into understanding all the life-giving implications of living as "a new creation" (2 Corinthians 5:17) as opposed to reinventing themselves according to their feelings. Listen carefully to the words of the kids you know and love. Identity formation is a conscious endeavor, and they're looking for guidance, particularly as it relates to sexuality and gender. Our students need to learn what it means to embrace the identity of "Christian," and everything that comes with it.

SECOND, WE MUST TEACH THE DOCTRINES OF GOD, HUMAN DEPRAVITY AND GOD'S GRACE.

One of the most personally liberating moments of my life came when someone explained to me, as a teenager, the grand plan of God's redemptive history—from Genesis to Revelation. Until that moment, I'd looked at the Scriptures as a kind of divinely-authored guidebook. It wasn't a unified whole, but rather a list of rules, regulations, and moral examples.

But when I saw the flow of redemptive history—Creation, Fall,

Redemption, and Restoration—it was like scales fell from my eyes! This was God's story, and in finding my place in God's story, I began to understand the majesty of God, my own slavery to sin, and my desperate need for God's grace.

Years later, my understanding of the nature and extent of the Fall and my corruption by sin has led to an increasingly robust theology of both human depravity and God's glorious and gracious work of salvation. Our world is broken. We are broken. Our default setting is to sin. And the one who whispered into our first parents' ears, "Did God really say…?", continues his efforts to derail us into self-worship and self-rule. So help your students to see and hear the enemy's voice as sober-minded and watchful (1 Peter 5:8–9) followers of Jesus, so that they might faithfully resist the enemy, listen to the Holy Spirit, and run into the grace-filled arms of God.

THIRD, NEVER STOP HELPING STUDENTS UNDERSTAND THAT THE CALL TO DISCIPLESHIP IS THE CALL TO AN INTEGRATED LIFE.

In recent years, I've heard more and more youth pastors justify their unwillingness to tackle some of the harder issues of the day by focusing on one ministry goal and one ministry goal alone: "I only want to see kids come to Jesus." Sounds good and noble, right? What this approach gets right is the invitation Jesus extends to broken and helpless sinners to "come as you are." But it ultimately fails because it de-emphasizes and even forgets the reality that Christ never follows "come as you are" with "stay as you are."

Sadly, many youth ministry "conversions" aren't to Jesus, but to something else—perhaps to a momentary, yet fleeting interest in Christianity. If Jesus is truly the Lord of all of life, then we cannot tolerate a dis-integrated faith. True regeneration and conversion always marries justification to sanctification. In other words, we must teach our kids that the correct response to God's mercy will cause us to worship God through living a counter-cultural life that is conformed to God's will and way (Romans 12:1–2).

Are we teaching what it means to be a Christian who integrates their faith into their academics, athletics, use of social media, relationships, sexuality, gender, etc.? The Christian faith speaks to all of life, and we fail our kids miserably when we don't teach, equip, and encourage them on the "hard way" (Matthew 7:13–14) of spiritual growth and maturity.

FOURTH, WE MUST TEACH THEM TO LIVE FAITHFULLY IN THE DIFFICULT NOW IN LIGHT OF THEIR GLORIOUS FUTURE HOPE.

Whenever I teach a class on youth culture, I always have my students interview a school teacher who has been engaged with students for at least two decades. Without fail, these tenured teachers lament a decline in resilience among their students. In their book *The Coddling of the American Mind: How Good Intentions and Bad Ideas Are Setting Up a Generation for Failure*, Greg Lukianoff and Jonathan Haidt identify what they call "The Untruth of Fragility" as one of the most dangerous lies of our times.

Here's the untruth: "What doesn't kill you makes you weaker."

Students avoid pain by avoiding difficulty because they fear any difficulty will undo them. But nothing could be further from the truth. Read the Bible from cover to cover, read church history, talk to saints who have had to endure difficulties, and we'll quickly see that God does good work in our lives when we are brought to the end of ourselves and we realize "the peaceable fruit of righteousness" (Hebrews 12:7–11). How else could the Psalmist say, "It is good for me that I was afflicted, that I might learn your statutes" (Psalm 119:71)?

Our students need to learn that difficulties in life, when we lean on the Lord to get through them, don't kill us or make us weaker. They make us stronger. To equip our students to effectively live to the glory of God in the now, we must teach them a rich theology of suffering. If our teens believe the lie that Jesus gives us a life that is void of pain, filled with pleasure, and always joyful, then they will quickly be disappointed and disillusioned. As the sobering statistics and anecdotal stories show, they will most likely walk away shaking their heads at all the unfulfilled promises.

Instead, the promise they need to believe is that God is with us through our earthly pain and suffering, using our circumstances for our good and his glory. His curriculum for our lives includes hard times that conform us to his image. James tells us to "count it all joy" through the trials that test our faith and produce steadfastness (James 1:2–4). Paul tells us our sufferings help us to groan for redemption. He tells us these present sufferings for Christ's sake (Philippians 1:29) cannot be compared to the glory that is to be revealed (Romans 8, 2 Corinthians 4:17–18).

Our kids need to hear *these truths* over the culture's constant untruths. They're growing up in a world where they're encouraged to live in the present moment without regard to the past or the future. They need to hear the full gospel and understand all the difficult realities of this temporary world even as they set their hearts and minds on the eternal blessed hope of the world to come.

THE HOW—MINISTRY PRACTICES

In his instructions to the Ephesians elders, the Apostle Paul told them to "Pay careful attention to yourselves and to all the flock, in which the Holy Spirit has made you overseers, to care for the church of God, which he obtained with his own blood" (Acts 20:28). No doubt, to pay careful attention involves faithful instruction in God's Word with an awareness that there will always be those who speak twisted things (Acts 20:29–30).

But care also must be taken regarding our ministry practices. Do they foster the growth of our individual students? Or do our practices confuse them? Could it be that the path to hell is paved with good youth ministry intentions?

Let me briefly encourage you to evaluate your ministry practices and correct course where necessary. Remember the goal: promote the advance of the gospel and the growth of your students into *resilient disciples*.

Here are three series of questions to consider.

1. In your church, are you creating an inter-generational

environment where your students have exposure to the full width and depth of the body of Christ? Or are you separating the generations and removing opportunities for the old and young to see each other first and foremost as mutually-edifying brothers and sisters in Christ? Sure, there are appropriate times for students to be engaged with their peers under the leadership of the youth ministry staff and volunteers. But consistently segregating the generations is counter-productive to effective ministry.

2. Does your youth ministry space create an environment for passive celebrity worship and performance? Or is it curated to facilitate active involvement and the building of community? As I've traveled and been in hundreds of youth ministry spaces over the years, I've seen that many churches have created youth spaces that look like concert venues. I've seen rooms with as few as twenty chairs set up facing a stage where a worship band and youth minister do the work of leading music and preaching while everyone else just watches. I'm not sure that place values the kind of interactions that will trump individualism and foster a participatory community.

3. Do you recognize the role parents play as those primarily responsible for the spiritual nurture of their children? Or have you consciously or unconsciously taken on that role by assuming philosophically and/or functionally that you can do a much better job than dad and mom? The Scriptures are clear that parents are primary (Deuteronomy 6, Ephesians 6), which means that the youth ministry is there to support and assist. Consider what Christian Smith says: "The empirical evidence is clear. In almost every case, no other institution or program comes close to shaping youth religiously as their parents do—not religious congregations, youth groups, faith-based schools, missions and service trips, summer camps, Sunday school, youth ministers, or anything else.

Those influences can reinforce the influence of parents, but almost never do they surpass or override it." Do everything you can to support, encourage, educate, and equip parents.

I am still haunted by a conversation I had with an influential youth pastor a few years ago. When I asked him about how he comes to conclusions on the big questions of life as a leader and teacher of kids, he responded, "I just follow my heart." Tears filled my eyes. I responded, "If I had chosen to live my life in this way, we wouldn't be having this conversation right now. I'd probably be in prison." Why would we ever allow emotions to direct our teaching and leading?

The prophet Jeremiah tells a truth that we see validated again and again through the stories we see in Scripture, on the news, in our friends, and, above all, in the mirror. Jeremiah says, "Cursed is the man who trusts in man and makes flesh his strength. ... Blessed is the man who trusts in the Lord, whose trust is the Lord. ... The heart is deceitful above all things, and desperately sick, who can understand it?" (Jeremiah 17)

Youth ministries must buck the spirit of the times and equip kids to reject the sovereignty of the deceitful and desperately sick self. We should focus on leading our kids into embracing a life of true freedom and true flourishing in obedience to the one true Sovereign God.

ABOUT THE AUTHOR

Walt Mueller is the founder and President of The Center for Parent/Youth Understanding (cpyu.org), an organization which endeavors to increase the ability of home and church to understand and respond to cultural trends in order to nurture children and teens into a lifetime of biblically-faithful, whole-life Christian discipleship. He's been in youth ministry for over four decades and is the host of the *Youth Culture Matters* long-form podcast, and the 1-minute daily *Youth Culture Today* podcast. He is the author of ten books, including his latest, *A Student's Guide to Navigating Culture* (Christian Focus, 2020).

You're a Pastor, Not a Therapist

Jeremy Pierre

INTRODUCTION

"I don't do therapy. I just preach the Word. If people listen, they'll be able to handle their own problems."

The words were clean and decisive, captivating the handful of pastors who'd asked the conference speaker out for breakfast. Around half-cleared plates and coffee mugs, everyone nodded their heads. I probably did so myself, though I remember feeling conflicted. I was a rookie pastor then and knew my experience was far less than this veteran's. Yet I couldn't get around the thought, *But people I know at your church are in therapy and you don't even know it.*

The tension I felt was between my belief in the power of the preached Word and my awareness that even people eager to receive the Word still struggle deeply with personal troubles. Years of pastoral ministry since have confirmed this tension. Here's what I've learned: Speaking the timeless Word to timebound individuals requires deep insight into both. To gain insight into Scripture, you have to study hard; to gain insight into individuals, you have to do the same.

A pastor is not a therapist. But that doesn't mean he opts out of helping folks with their personal troubles. In fact, a pastor is tasked with helping in ways a therapist isn't. In this article, I'll explain what I mean by this. A pastor's job is not to dismiss personal experience, but rather to help people see it differently—specifically, to see it according to who God is and the chief purpose of his design for human life.

PEOPLE WANT TO UNDERSTAND THEIR OWN EXPERIENCE.

People see therapists to make sense out of their own experience. This is not in itself a problem. The problem is that therapeutic models have largely emerged from a secular culture characterized by a deep valuing of what Carl Truman describes as *expressive individualism*. Human experience is understood not from the external reference point of sacred order, but rather from the internal reference point of perceived happiness.[29]

29 Carl R. Trueman, *The Rise and Triumph of the Modern Self: Cultural Amnesia, Expressive Individualism, and the Road to Sexual Revolution* (Wheaton, IL: Crossway, 2020), 46.

Generally speaking, therapy is the attempt to help a person live effectively and consistently according to that perception of wholeness. My purpose here is not to argue the benefits and drawbacks of various therapeutic models. I'm merely pointing out what therapy as an enterprise is trying to do.

A pastor is not a therapist. But that does not mean he overlooks personal experience. Rather, it means he helps people see their experience from a much broader perspective—how God designed people to relate to himself and to his sacred ordering of creation. God designed people to love him and others (Matt 22:37-40), and this design purpose is how we understand healthy functioning. It is the great privilege of human experience—a privilege restored to humanity by God himself becoming a man (Heb 2:10-11). The redemptive work of Jesus is the only way to ultimately make sense of human experience. This includes an individual's personal experience, too.

PASTORS ADDRESS PERSONAL EXPERIENCE AS NEITHER

UNIMPORTANT NOR ALL-IMPORTANT.

Your job as a pastor is neither to overlook the importance of personal experience nor to venerate it as sacred. Pastors can commit both errors.

As in the opening example, I've seen pastors dismiss the experiences of their people because those experiences seem odd, unsettling, or "worldly." Dismissal is almost guaranteed to send your people looking to others who will help them understand themselves. And we rob our people of the explanatory power of the Word for personal experience. The biblical authors themselves don't ignore individual experience, but address it in light of higher realities. When Jesus spoke to the woman at the well, he did so as if her domestic situation mattered. Peter's occupation as a fisherman mattered. Timothy's stomach problems mattered. The false teaching threatening the church in Galatia as opposed to what was threatening the church in Corinth mattered. As a pastor, you should never imply, *Your unique experience doesn't matter. Truth does.* Instead, make it clear that *Truth helps you understand how your unique experience matters.*

I've seen pastors commit the other error, too. They get caught up in a person's experience and feel uneasy offering commentary. They don't want to seem dismissive, so they unknowingly affirm the person's bad takes on everything from what it means to be happy to how they see themselves. Pastors can fear being seen as the trite "Bible answers" guy that they neglect their duty to actually speak solid ideas from Scripture, helping a person begin to see their experience in the light of God's kindness, faithfulness, and redemptive intentions in their unique situation. Pastors should not imply, *Your unique experience is all that matters. Truth can wait.* They should rather say, *Truth helps you experience more fully who God made you to be.*

So how do you address human experience well? By setting it in its proper order.

PASTORS HELP THEIR PEOPLE SEE THEMSELVES

IN RELATION TO GOD AND TO HIS SACRED ORDER.

Pastors say to their people, *You were made to see yourself as God sees you, not as you prefer to be seen.* God's first conversation with Adam was about Adam's identity, telling him who he was and what he'd been designed to do (Gen 1:28). Adam needed words from God to make sense of himself. That's true of all people created in God's image. They don't know how they fit into the order of things without God revealing it to them.

That's why the rest of creation can be described as the *sacred order.* The holy God designed creation to reflect his holiness. He ordered creation to reflect the truth of his own mind and the beauty of his own character. He then placed individuals within that order. This means truth and beauty are not subjectively determined by individuals. In other words, you don't understand yourself truly apart from the sacred order in which you were placed.[30]

30 Ibid., 194.

This is why a pastor always has his Bible open. It's not to ignore what a person describes of his own experience, but rather to be able to say, *Your unique experience matters, and is only rightly understood in light of truths revealed from outside you. Let's consider a few.* And then, he unpacks one or two of the countless themes in Scripture that illuminate different aspects of what a person is going through. None of it is to dismiss personal experience, but to illuminate it.

PASTORS ACCOMPLISH THIS THROUGH BOTH PUBLIC AND PERSONAL MINISTRIES OF THE WORD.

The public and personal ministries of the Word complement one another in this task. Together, they create an alternate social imaginary, an eternal perspective based on what God has revealed in his Word.

Public ministry of the Word, primarily preaching, should address the common experience of the people. Pastors should challenge themselves to consider what their people face in their range of professions, trades, social circles, educational settings, and neighborhoods. Be around your people in many different settings—their workplaces, their homes, their activities. Then, as a pastor studies to achieve insight into the meaning of a text, he will view his people's collective experience in a new light. This allows him to apply the text for them with greater insight.

Personal ministry of the Word, including mentorship and counseling, should regularly address the personal experiences of individuals. This takes more back-and-forth. It takes listening and knowing an individual and addressing his or her specific experience, not just collective experiences. Not all pastors will be equally gifted for such exploratory conversations, but seeking to gain insight into the personal experiences of your people will give you opportunity to apply Scripture with greater specificity and effectiveness.

Pastor, you're not a therapist. You hold a longer-term position in the lives of your people. You aren't just helping them for a short time to accomplish specific personal goals. Rather, you are helping them over a lifetime to understand themselves in light of what God says about them.

ABOUT THE AUTHOR

Jeremy Pierre is the dean of students and associate professor of biblical counseling at The Southern Baptist Theological Seminary and serves as an elder at Clifton Baptist Church.

Church Discipline and Expressive Individualism

Jonathan Parnell

E xpressive individualism, the phrase coined by philosopher Charles
Taylor in *A Secular Age*, captures the largest ideological shift in
America during the twentieth century. It represents the cumulative
effect of secularism's insatiable appetite to understand the self. Two other
phrases coined by Taylor provide some background.

The first is "exclusive humanism," the idea that humans are exclusively
responsible for the happenings in our world. This idea, on a societal level,
cuts off any true contact with transcendence. Exclusive humanism means
humans on their own, without God.

This leads to a second phrase—the "immanent frame." This is Taylor's term for a "constructed social space where instrumental rationali-
ty is a key value." In other words, humans who have abandoned God still
long for meaning, and if that meaning can't be found in transcendence,
then it must be found in what is immanent—in what is *here*, accessible,
earthly. The immanent frame infuses depth in material things, but in isolation from the Creator that exclusive humanism denies. The immanent

frame requires that *the things of this world must be special.*

This is the thinking behind our society's fairly recent infatuation with "organic," "hand-crafted," "home-made," and so forth. Take a look in your pantry and notice the plethora of these buzz words. Remember that ideas influence the market, but then the market drives ideas. We're largely comfortable in the immanent frame because it sells, and that's finally what gives way to expressive individualism.

If exclusive humanism (i.e., a world without God) leads to the immanent frame (i.e., searching for meaning in the immanent, where we do have contact), then the burden for finding that meaning falls on the individual, which is what our society means when you hear talk of "finding your own way," or "doing your own thing," or "you do you." This is expressive individualism.

INFILTRATING EVERYTHING

Since we've done away with God, we need to find our own "origin story." The individual must construct his own meaning, and then publicize it. And it's especially in the publicity that the individual is fulfilled because the publicity is immanent and accessible—*coram populo.*

Carl Trueman then takes sociologist Philip Rieff's idea of the "psychological man," who lives to attend to his own inner self, and combines it with Charles Taylor's expressive individualism. "You do you" is the result, and that only counts if you're letting everybody know about the "you." It's not hard to see how social media has intensified the game—again, chasing the idea, but also driving it.

The way this idea has touched everything is stunning. I'm confronted with it each time I put on a pair of St. Louis Cardinals dress socks, grab my St. Louis Cardinals coffee mug, and hop into my car that has a St. Louis Cardinals decal. There's also the mousepad, the key chain, and even of course my Bitmoji—a digital avatar of myself wearing a St. Louis Cardinals ballcap and t-shirt. I own all of this because, personally, I'm a fan of the St. Louis Cardinals. The forms of expression are almost endless, even for just one little detail about my self-understanding.

While not everything to do with the expressive individual is nefarious, neither the aspects of selfhood nor the forms of expression stay as benign as a Cardinals coffee mug. Expressive individualism has infiltrated the deeps—most notably seen in our society's confusion over sexuality. The tectonic plates of our humanity have shifted as the modern self has triumphed. All of this has accompanied a deep suspicion and even aversion to church membership generally and church discipline in particular.

So now we come to the real topic.

FIRST, CHURCH MEMBERSHIP

The high calling of the local church is to officially affirm and shape the regenerate individual's life in Christ. Membership in a local church, as Jonathan Leeman describes it, "is a formal relationship between a church and a Christian characterized by the church's affirmation and oversight of a Christian's discipleship and the Christian's submission to living out his or her discipleship in the care of the church."

This care includes the continual affirmation that the Christian is indeed a *Christian*, expressed by the church's attentiveness to the Christian's confession of the gospel and conduct consistent with that confession. Dependent upon the Scriptures, the church vouches that the individual is a Christian because they believe rightly and live rightly.

Therefore, for a Christian to even join a local church—or rather, to *submit* to a local church—they must directly renounce expressive individualism by accepting the church's role in announcing and shaping their public "identity".

For pastors, explaining this counter-cultural reality of church membership is the first step to teaching our people the necessity of church discipline. When Jesus is worshiped rather than self, and when membership of a body is rightly understood in contrast to expressive individualism, then the actions required to restore wayward members and guard the church's purity make sense (see 1 Corinthians 12:18–20).

THE AUDACITY OF DISCIPLINE

What happens when a member's "inward quest for personal psychological happiness" contradicts the teaching of Scripture? Who decides whether that's true? Who has the authority?

By becoming a church member, an individual Christian relinquishes to the church the authority to discern whether one's conduct is sinful, as guided by the Bible. The individual effectively says, "I'm no longer an independent authority unto myself. I invite the church in." For example, imagine that a church member abandons his spouse because he finds the marriage no longer fulfilling. He's convinced that Jesus desires his personal fulfillment above all things, and so he walks away from his marital vows, disobeying Ephesians 5:22–33. What's really happening here is that the member is forsaking Jesus to serve self, and it's the church's responsibility to exhort the member to stop. On the authority of God's revealed will in Scripture, the church judges this member to be sinning and takes the necessary steps of correction, whether the member agrees with the judgment or not.

Increasingly, though, the mindset of expressive individualism tempts Christians to disagree with the church's judgment or even count such confrontations as sinful. In many cases, the individual will find a way to justify his behavior on the grounds of what Trueman calls an "anarchic emotive morality." Expressive individualism cares less about unrepentant sin and more about the unrepentant audacity of the church to judge behavior sinful when the individual disagrees.

THE NEED FOR COMPASSION AND COURAGE

These days, pastors are desperate for wisdom from above in order to be wise as serpents and innocent as doves (see James 3:17; Matthew 10:16). Compassion and courage have always been relevant to the pastoral calling, but perhaps especially today, in two particular applications.

Regarding compassion, we must remember the difference between the deceivers and the deceived.

Most of our church members who buy into the most tragic manifestations of expressive individualism have been led astray. They're the deceived. Pastors should not let their frustration over an ideology like expressive individualism turn into a frustration with everyone influenced by that ideology. Compassion affords patience, and we should give individuals ample room to hear the church's correction and welcome its discipleship.

Regarding courage, we should prepare for discipline situations to raise larger criticisms related to church authority and the validity of discipline. Yet we must not let that deter us from obeying God (see Acts 5:32). There will likely be discipline situations in your church that lead to public criticisms. When the church of Jesus Christ undermines the god of self and exercises discipline, the expressive individual sometimes takes to Twitter for expression. The internet will shake its fist; your church will be misrepresented; and you'll know that it all could have been avoided if your church let that member continue down their ruinous road of sin. But what is right is rarely popular, and in this climate it takes uncanny, Spirit-led courage for the church to say to individuals "That is sin." God help us.

ABOUT THE AUTHOR

Jonathan Parnell is the lead pastor of Cities Church in Saint Paul, Minnesota, where he lives with his wife, Melissa, and their eight children.

The Ordinances: A True and Better Identity Politics

Bobby Jamieson

B y common consent, identity politics is tearing people apart. At bottom, identity politics starts with some feature that differentiates people into a group and forms political perspectives, alliances, and goals that advance the interest of the group. Race and gender are by far the most common organizing principles of identity politics, but they aren't the only ones. These days, nearly anything can get turned into a badge of identity, a lever to elevate one group at the expense of another.

Identity politics hardens differences into divides. It politicizes everything. It can easily turn loyalty to your group into loathing of every competing group. Often, it implicitly sets up some standard of who gets to count as fully human, a standard that your group possesses and the other does not. Identity politics turns common life into a war of every socially constructed subcommunity against every other.

So its problems are obvious. But identity politics doesn't just create problems "out there": many of the forces that threaten to pull churches apart are driven by toxic, worldly manifestations of identity politics.

One reason that political disagreements between Christians so often escalate into battle royales is that it increasingly seems like disagreeing with my view is disparaging my person or my people.

What's the alternative? What can unearth and uproot and undermine the unbiblical assumptions that animate identity politics and threaten to tear apart what God has joined together?

I would submit a simple, perhaps surprisingly obvious answer: baptism and the Lord's Supper.

Every group identity derives its political power from its answer to the questions:

- Where are we from?
- Where are we going?
- To whom do we belong?

Consider how the ordinances of baptism and the Lord's Supper answer those for every Christian, and how they construct an alternative identity politics. One might even say, a true and better identity politics.

WHERE ARE WE FROM?

Baptism tells us that we are from the grave (Rom. 6:1–4; Col. 2:11–12). Before we were united to Christ, we were the living dead. We had no spiritual life in us and deserved nothing but death. Baptism reminds us that, no matter what earthly advantages or disadvantages any of us had before coming to Christ, none of us had any claim on God, any standing before him, or any power to alter our condition.

WHERE ARE WE GOING?

Baptism not only dramatizes our spiritual death; it also previews the resurrection that our faith in Christ guarantees. Because Christ was raised from the dead, and we're united to him by faith, we too will be raised with him, and his resurrection power is already at work in us by his Spirit. Baptism reminds us that our proper and permanent home is the new creation.

And the Lord's Supper reminds us that our final destination is a celebration in which all God's people will partake. "I tell you I will not drink again of this fruit of the vine until that day when I drink it new with you in my Father's kingdom" (Matt. 26:29). This side of paradise, every utopia will fail. No political program can perfect humanity. But the certain destination of all God's people is a never-ending celebration, in perfect peace with God and perfect harmony with all his people.

TO WHOM DO WE BELONG?

Both baptism and the Lord's Supper proclaim that we belong to God, and, because we belong to God, we also belong to each other. When Jesus commands his disciples to baptize new believers "in the name" of the Father and Son and Holy Spirit, he is saying that baptism is a badge of belonging (Matt. 28:19). Baptism marks off a believer as the personal property of the Triune God. And because baptism makes us God's property, it also makes us each other's family. Those who were baptized at Pentecost were, by that act, "added to the church" (Acts 2:41). Baptism creates a new body politic, one defined not by any prior criterion of group membership, but by repentance and faith in Christ.

And the Lord's Supper corporately enacts our communion with Christ and thereby our communion with each other. That is, in the Lord's Supper, a local church, by faith, shares in the benefits of Christ together (1 Cor. 10:16). And by so sharing in Christ, we come to share a single common life. By partaking of the bread that stands for his body, we ourselves solidify into solidarity: "Because there is one bread, we who are many are one body, for we all partake of the one bread" (1 Cor 10:17).

Baptism and the Lord's Supper proclaim to us the true narrative of who we are and whose we are, of where we've come from and where we're going. When any Christian asks, "Who am I?" baptism and the Lord's Supper return the ultimate shorthand answers. Baptism and the Lord's Supper declare that what unites us in Christ is both more fundamental and more ultimate than anything that threatens to divide us.

What difference should that make as you seek to pastor, or live as a faithful member of, a local church? Here's one application out of hundreds: When you disagree with another Christian over some matter of political philosophy or policy or advocacy, place your disagreement on one scale and baptism and the Lord's Supper on the other. Is your disagreement of such gravity that you could not celebrate the Lord's Supper with this other professing Christian? Is their error so great, as you see it, that you think their baptism invalid? If not, make sure that you conduct your controversy with that believer—its tone, matter, extent, and consequences—in light of the more fundamental and more ultimate realities that unite you.

ABOUT THE AUTHOR

Bobby Jamieson is an associate pastor of Capitol Hill Baptist Church in Washington, DC. He is the author, most recently, of Jesus' Death and Heavenly Offering in Hebrews. You can find him on Twitter at @bobby_jamieson.

Raising Children in an Age of Expressive Individualism

Abigail Dodds

Perhaps one of the great needs of our cultural moment is to consider the ways we, as moms and dads, have succumbed to the cultural winds of our era and how we may have left our children exposed to those harsh and deadly gale force gusts. Would our acceptance of certain cultural norms be shocking to Christians from other eras? Our movie choices? Our narcissistic tendencies? Our luxury beliefs? Our lack of conviction over biblical truth? Our lack of obedience to biblical commands?

Every generation has weaknesses and blind spots, but today's Christian moms and dads are facing a world of expressive individualism in all its varied and sundry forms—–from an obsession with one's so-called gender as the defining self-demarcation to an obsession with personality tests to define one's core inner self. The world is awash in self-identity and the need to express it far and wide.

This is why parents must be relentless as they evaluate whether this trend has taken hold—or more likely, to what degree it has taken hold—in themselves. Ruthlessly cut it out; ruthlessly reject yourself and your sense of things as the center of the universe; ruthlessly deny any desire to express a godless inner thought life for public consumption. Be who you are: a Christian who belongs to God, who was bought with a price, whose inner and outer self are meant to glorify God.

Then, we must turn to our children and guide them in the way they should go. Here are three principles to help inoculate your children from expressive individualism—an ideology that holds each person's core self is an inner psychological self based on inner feelings and desires that ought to be lived out and expressed—and all its ensuing ills.

1. HELP THEM SEE THAT WHO THEY ARE IS DISCERNIBLE AND GIVEN TO THEM, NOT MYSTERIOUS AND CHOSEN BY THEM.

Expressive individualism wants to locate the "true self" deep inside the folds of the belly button, where all great mysteries reside. But finding out "who you are" is really very simple. Children must be taught to observe their God-given body. Is it male or female? That tells you something profound about who you are and what you were made for. It tells you if you are daughter or son, sister or brother, uncle or aunt, potential wife or husband, potential mother or father. Being made male or female is an assignment directly from the hand of God himself and it is to be received with joy.

Furthermore, hopefully your children are in Christ, which means they are his servants, his brothers and sisters, his friends. And so they are sons and daughters of God the Father. These are the deepest answers we have for the most important questions of identity. Without this, children will be left to drudge up paltry meaning from made-up gender identities, online tribes, and narcissistic social media traps that make them spectators of their own life's meaning and popularity (or lack thereof).

There are other ways of discerning in a more temporary way "who you are." Are you school age? Then you are a student. Do you have a job? Then you are an employee. These titles may come and go, but they are important indicators of who we are at any given time and what we are meant to be doing with ourselves. We must teach our children that who they are is not a mystery, it is a discernible gift, and it comes with certain duties and joys that are fitting to the circumstance.

As parents, we must protect our children from those who would teach them otherwise. There is nothing less than the eternal well-being of our children at stake. It is our obligation to make truth the norm. It is their obligation to listen to us and obey us. But none of that can happen if moms and dads opt out by allowing their children to be indoctrinated into the ways of the world.

2. HELP THEM SEE THAT WHAT THEY *DO* REVEALS THE HEART, OFTEN MORE THAN WHAT THEY *FEEL*.

In the parable of the two sons, Jesus tells of a Father who told his sons to work in the vineyard for the day. One said he would go but didn't. The other said he wouldn't go but changed his mind and went. It was the one who went to the vineyard who did the will of his father. Likewise, our actions are a meaningful indicator of what we truly believe. Our beliefs are not off in some theoretical, talk-only, feelings-make-meaning realm.

Our beliefs are made genuine with hands and feet and minds that serve the Lord. In today's anxiety-ridden society, children need to be reminded that belief-fueled action is how we do God's will—and that God's will is a safe place to be. Our children need to be taught that because the Lord is mindful of them, because he cares so sovereignly and completely for them, they are free to focus their thoughts and their actions on other things—things like God, his excellencies, his Word, the good of their family and friends, the service of the church, the spread of the gospel, and the help of those in need. They are free to obey.

3. HELP THEM TRUST EXTERNAL REALITY— GOD'S SPIRIT, GOD'S WORD, AND GOD'S PEOPLE—RATHER THAN GOING IT ALONE WITH

THEIR INNER SENSE OF THINGS.

The biggest way to help your children trust God is to actually trust him yourself—to actually be banking on his promises day by day, to know them, to read them, to put all your hope in them, and to do so regularly as a family and in the company of the local church. These habits of grace, as David Mathis calls them, make for godly muscle memory that will serve as a protection in times to come.

What does your family do in a crisis, big or small? Pray and remember God's promises. What does your family do after dinner each night? Read the Bible and pray for one another's requests. What does your family do on Sunday mornings and Wednesday nights? Gather with God's people to sing, learn, fellowship, pray, baptize, share the Lord's Supper, and generally just love one another. There is nothing more powerfully protective for our children than rhythms of dependence on God. These rhythms help them know where to look for help—look outside yourself! Look to Christ, to his Spirit, to his Spirit's words, and to his people.

We cannot depend on our inner sense of things as an infallible guide—it does guide, but it must be calibrated by his Word and taken captive to Christ. Lord willing, our children will have years of practice listening to the Spirit, identifying false teaching, submitting their own thought life to the Lord, and enjoying the freedom of an identity given by God the Father, not conjured out of a vacuous navel-lint ego. There is no more important work in the universe for moms and dads than to train their children in the Lord, to talk with them as you drive down the road, while you make coffee in the morning, and as you start the bedtime routine. Our children need us attentive and equipped, providing the stability of Christ as they grow up, so that they too can find their feet in these tumultuous days.

ABOUT THE AUTHOR

Abigail Dodds is a wife, mother of five, and graduate of Bethlehem College & Seminary.

The Pastor and an Unmessianic Sense of Non Destiny

Carl Trueman

For many men of a certain age, the mid-life crisis is just that: a mid-life crisis, a time for despairing that youth, good looks, and perhaps hair have gone, never to return. For me, however, the experience has been pretty positive so far: not only have I been able to hand on my old banger of car to my oldest son (thus making myself the greatest dad in the world), but I've also broken with my lifelong habit of driving pieces of junk until they disintegrate and purchased an inexpensive but decent sports car. Not quite sure how my wife let me get away with it; but the fact that my previous car leaked when it rained and the present Mrs. T had told me that enough was enough and she was no longer prepared to "be dripped on" as we drove along in a storm one day, seemed to open up a great opportunity for sneaking a good car onto the driveway. As she rolled her eyes, she did say to me that a husband with a decent looking car is, from her perspective, better than one with a secret girlfriend and/or a not-so-secret toupee. I had to agree: there are indeed much worse forms of the mid-life crisis (MLC) out there.

One other aspect of my MLC, and one that I have found extraordinarily helpful, is the death of ambition which, in my experience, it seems to have brought in its wake. The realization that one cannot be the best at everything, or even those things at which one used to be the best, is presumably a factor in quite a few MLCs—and for me this was a welcome liberation. I woke up one day a few years ago at the age of forty, and realized that, if I was hit by a bus that night, whatever academic contribution I was ever going to make had already been made; I had done it; I need not worry about it anymore. I could, of course, continue grinding the stuff out, like some intellectual sausage machine, but it would be more of the same, variations on a theme I had already played. No, an early Trueman death would not deprive the world of some great insight it might otherwise miss. I knew I would continue to write and even to do research, but I would do these for the pleasure I found in them, not because I believed it was my God-given task to enrich the waiting world with my pearls of wisdom.

This inner peace reminded me a little of the mental health statistics when I was at university. These indicated that good mental health was generally strongest among us intellectual middle-of-the-packers who were happy with whatever results we achieved: if we scored high, that was a bonus; if we crashed to earth, that was a bit of a blow but nothing too serious; we sailed on in our own, carefree way, not allowing work to interfere too much with trips to the pub, the odd game of darts or pool, and the general enjoyment of life. By contrast, breakdowns and suicides were most common among the intellectually brilliant high-fliers, those for whom nothing less than perfection was acceptable.

So it is with the MLC brigade. There are those for whom the diminution of their intellect, musculature, looks, and hair is a traumatic and desperate experience; and they find nothing which seems to compensate. You can point to the growth of hair in nostrils and ears as much as you like, but—trust me—these men will take no consolation from the fact that their overall number of active follicles remains relatively stable.

For me, and I hope for others, being on the cusp of middle age has, contrary to the above, proved liberating. The key, I believe, is to match diminishing abilities and opportunities with diminishing ambition; balance the former with the latter, and you achieve a sort of zen consciousness where middle age does not seem so terrible after all.

Of course, the acquisition of such consciousness is really somewhat counter-cultural: not only does today's world consider ageing, and the inevitable physical weakening that comes with it, as sins; it also teaches us that everyone is special, has a particularly unique contribution to make, and must have a prize of some kind. Everyone needs to tell the world about their greatness, their uniqueness. It reminds me of the legendary football manager, Brian Clough, who, when asked if he was the best manager in the world famously replied, "No, but I'm somewhere in the top one." He was funny because he was one of a kind. But we're all Cloughs now, with the cultural term for those who lack confidence in their unique brilliance being, so I believe, "loser."

This belief that we are each special is, by and large, complete tosh. Most of us are mediocre, make unique contributions only in the peculiar ways we screw things up, and could easily be replaced as husband, father, or employee by somebody better suited to the task. The mythology nevertheless helps to sell things and allows us to feel good about ourselves; indeed, the older you get, the more things it sells, from gym memberships, to cosmetic surgery, to hair pieces, to botox injections. But it is just mythology—the whole of human history so far strongly suggests that, as you get old, you cease to be as cool, and that you inevitably find that life just isn't as sweet as it was when you were eighteen.

As I look around the church, it strikes me that this zen-like condition of a lack of ambition is much to be desired because far too many Christians have senses of destiny which verge on the messianic. The confidence that the Lord has a special plan and purpose just for them shapes the way they act and move. Now, just for the record, I am a good Calvinist, and I certainly believe each individual has a destiny; what concerns me is the way in which our tendency to think of ourselves as special and unique bleeds over into a sense of special destiny whereby the future, or at least the future of myself, comes to be the priority and to trump all else.

Put bluntly, when I read the Bible it seems to me that the church is the meaning of human history. But it is the church, a corporate body, not the distinct individuals who go to make up her membership. Of course, all of us individuals have our gifts and our roles to play: the Lord calls us each by name and numbers the very hairs of our heads. But to borrow Paul's analogy of the body, we have no special destiny in ourselves taken as isolated units, anymore than bits of our own bodies do in isolation from each other. When I act, I act as a whole person; my hand has no special role of its own; it acts only in the context of being part of my overall body. With the church, the destiny of the whole is greater than the sum of the destinies of individual Christians.

This is an important insight which should profoundly shape our thinking and, indeed, our praying. My special destiny as a believer is to be part of the church; and it is the church that is the big player in God's wider plan, not me. That puts me, my uniqueness, my importance, my role, in definite perspective. The problem today is that too many have the idea that God's primary plan is for them, and the church is secondary, the instrument to the realization of their individual significance. They may not even realize they think that way, but like those involuntary "tells" during a poker game, so certain unconscious spiritual behaviors give the game away.

Take, for example, prayer. Compare the "O Lord, please use me for doing X" variety with the priorities of the Lord's Prayer, where the petitions are much more modest: "Lead me not into temptation, deliver me from evil, for the kingdom is yours, etc." One could paraphrase that prayer perhaps as follows: "Lord, keep me out of trouble and don't let me get in the way of the growth of your kingdom." The Lord's Prayer, by contrast with many prayers we cook up for ourselves, is a great example of words designed for the lips of believers who really understand the gospel, of those with, to coin a phrase, an unmessianic sense of non-destiny.

Now think about church commitment. Many churches require members to take vows when they join, one of which usually requires submission to the authority of elders and a commitment to the local body. This is surely the church vow which is as casually taken as it is regularly broken. How many Christians move membership from one church to another as soon as their pet issue or problem is not addressed, or because they see a better option elsewhere? And I haven't even mentioned the countless Christians who attend churches but never formally join. Once you shift membership from one church for no reason other than it doesn't scratch your itch, it becomes a whole lot easier to do it again—and again, and again. But if you have an unmessianic sense of non-destiny, this is unlikely to be a problem: you won't consider yourself important enough to justify breaking a solemn, public vow.

The West worships the individual. From the cradle to the grave, it tells us all how special and unique we are, how vital we are to everything, how there's a prize out there just for us. Well, the world turned for thousands of years before any of us showed up; it will continue turning long after we've gone, short of the parousia; and even if you, me, or the Christian next door are tonight hit by an asteroid, kidnapped by aliens, or sucked down the bathroom plughole, very little will actually change; even our loved ones will somehow find a way to carry on without us. We really are not that important. So let's drop the pious prayers which translate roughly as "Lord, how can a special guy/gal like myself help you out some?" and pray rather that the Lord will grow his kingdom despite our continual screw ups, that he will keep us from knocking over the furniture, and that, when all is said and done, somehow, by God's grace, we will finish well despite our best efforts to the contrary.

MLCs are dreaded by many men, but my advice is: gents, seize with both hands the opportunity to truly grasp that, whatever you thought at age eighteen, you are not actually the messiah and you have no special destiny which sets you apart from everybody else. The former is Christ alone; the latter is primarily reserved for his church. We all need to cultivate that certain unmessianic sense of non-destiny which will make us better citizens of the kingdom.

EDITOR'S NOTE

This article originally appeared on Carl's blog in 2010.

ABOUT THE AUTHOR

Carl Trueman is a Professor of Biblical and Religious Studies at Grove City College in Grove City, Pennsylvania.

"You've Got Self:"

HOW THE INTERNET CULTIVATES EXPRESSIVE INDIVIDUALISM IN ALL OF US

Samuel D. James

C hristopher Nolan's 2010 film *Inception* tells a story about a technology called "dream-sharing," invented at some indeterminate point in the future, that allows participants to enter into one another's dreams via their subconscious. The main character, played by Leonardo DiCaprio, assembles a team of dream "hackers" to invade the mind of a billionaire business heir and convince his subconscious to break up his father's commercial empire. In one of the film's mostly subtly metaphorical scenes, the team visits a chemist who can make an especially potent sedative to allow for vivid and prolonged dream-sharing. The chemist takes the team downstairs, where they're led to a dimly lit room where dozens of people are sleeping, connecting to dream sharing devices. The chemist explains that these people come to spend hours every day dreaming together, as their subconscious selves construct an alternative life in their dreams. Stunned, the team asks, "They come here to fall asleep?" "No," the chemist replies. "They come here to wake up." The dream has become their reality.

There are no real-world dream sharing devices, but there is one real-world technology that connects billions of people in a dream-reality: the Internet.

As Carl Trueman brilliantly lays out in *The Rise and Triumph of the Modern Self*, expressive individualism has its origins in a complex collision of history, philosophy, and politics. Today, however, the most powerful vehicle for shaping people in its image is not the classroom or Supreme Court, but the Internet. To see this more clearly, we need to think of the Internet less as a singular tool or hobby, and more like what it is now: an immersive epistemological habitat in which hundreds of millions of people have regular, active membership. The Internet has transformed the way humans read, learn, communicate, labor, shop, recreate, and even "worship." No other technology is as disruptive to traditional forms of human activity.

Membership in the online commons has formative effects on us, just like membership in a local church. The liturgies of assembled, embodied, gospel worship point us toward one set of beliefs and values, while the liturgies of Internet membership point us toward a different set.

While secular technology critics have been talking this way about digital life for a while, Christians largely have not. Instead, we've focused not on the form of the Internet, but on its content, encouraging one another to avoid pornography, slander, and envy on the various website and social media platforms we navigate daily. This encouragement is good and necessary, but much more is needed. Pastors and church leaders in particular need to see online technologies as powerful instruments of personal formation that push us in a certain spiritual and epistemological direction.

Before going further, we should take careful note of something important. The Bible's vision of human flourishing as divine image-bearers and Christ-followers is a deeply analog vision. By this I mean that Scripture both assumes and prescribes doctrines, attitudes, and practices that are tied to our embodied, physical existence. For one thing, Christians believe that divine revelation is expressed in a physical book, the Bible, and that this book features language with objective meaning.[31] Further, the very first thing we learn from the Bible about ourselves is that we are created in the image of God, male and female. This means that our fundamental identity as people is tied to our bodies. God creates physical image-bearers who have embodied sexual identities, and in submission to God these image-bearers come together to marry, make love, and bear children that fill the earth (with their physical selves) and subdue it. Family is not an abstract concept, but a flesh-and-blood institution that is ordered according to real, embodied persons.

The Internet, by contrast, is radically disembodied. To be online is, in a very real sense, to escape the givenness of created existence. The social critic Laurence Scott writes:

> If our bodies have traditionally provided the basic outline of our presence in the world, then we can't enter a networked environment, in which we present ourselves in multiple places at once, without rethinking the scope and limits of embodiment. While we sit next to one person, smiling through a screen at someone else, our thoughts, our visions, our offhand and heartfelt declarations materialize in the fragments in one another's pockets. It's astonishing to think how in the last twenty years the limits and coherence of our bodies have been so radically redefined.[32]

The Internet's disembodied, "fragmented" character is not merely interesting trivia. It is a massively important part of the way being online shapes our beliefs, intuitions, and habits.

Consider now three distinct "digital liturgies" that shape all of us in the image of the disembodied Internet.[33]

1. "MY STORY, MY TRUTH"

Online technology's flattening, democratizing character means that

---

31 By "objective" I do not mean to underestimate the difficulty of discerning meaning or the role of interpretation. I simply mean that the language in the Bible is real language, put there by rational humans, and discernible by the same.

32 Laurence Scott, *The Four-Dimensional Human: Ways of Being in the Digital World.* (New York: W.W. Norton, 2015), 4

33 Portions of this section are adapted from an essay I wrote for Desiring God, "Constantly (Dis)Connected" https://www.desiringgod.org/articles/constantly-disconnected

the most valuable social currency is not expertise, wisdom, or character, but story. When a truth claim goes up against a narrative, the narrative wins every time. Personal experience is the authoritative norm in digital discourse, and in many cases no amount of evidence or argument can trump it. To suggest that someone's story may be relevant but not necessarily authoritative is often seen as a grossly unacceptable attack on their personhood.

The power of individual story to provide justification for desires and thwart any criticism is powerfully evident to Gen-Z. In her book *Irreversible Damage: The Transgender Craze Seducing Our Daughters*, journalist Abigail Shrier describes how large and growing numbers of teen and preteen Americans are learning to question their given gender through transgendered influencers, particularly on YouTube, Reddit, and Tumblr. The influencers differ in personality and approach, but one message virtually all of them have in common is: Don't listen to anyone who tells you that you aren't trans. They don't know and can't understand.

When coupled with the immersive, disembodied character of the Internet, this is an enormously powerful message. The Internet requires constant curation, which means that online existence can and must be continually tweaked so that nothing that convicts or unnerves us need be seen. Social media algorithms encourage users to go deeper into their wildest and most fringe interests, because it is those interests that fuel prolonged activity on the app. And all of this descent into the depths of our own emotional and psychological states happens away from the observation and help of others in our lives, as the technology isolates us and digital culture insists that it alone is a safe place for us.

But according to Scripture, neither you nor I are the final interpreters of our own experience. Rather, we are finite creatures with limited vision. Our experiences certainly matter, but they are not ultimate. Because we belong to a Creator rather than ourselves, it is his Story that infuses meaning into ours. His Story reveals a meaning to our lives that we receive and instead of create, including a redemptive meaning to our suffering. His Story also places us in a community of people close to us, not "influencers" with a lifestyle to sell, but fathers, mothers, brothers, and sisters by whom we truly are seen and known.

2. "IF IT DOESN'T FEEL TRUE, IT'S PROBABLY NOT"

As the internet has escaped its physical tethers and become a mobile, ambient habitat, it has altered not only our sense of self but our sense of truth. By continually stressing our reservoirs of attention, digital culture primes us to form our beliefs based on immediate intuition. Our desire to think deeply is compromised by the internet's tyrannical novelty and immediacy, and as our desire to think deeply gives way, so does our ability.

This was the conclusion of Nicholas Carr in his monumental 2010 book *The Shallows: What the Internet Is Doing to Our Brains*, which every pastor should read. Carr presents compelling evidence that the kind of reading and learning we do online is very different than the kind we do offline, and that the Internet is by its nature an epistemological architecture that conditions us away from deep thinking. "The Net is, by design," Carr writes, "an interruption system, a machine geared for dividing attention."

Psychological research long ago proved what most of us know from experience: frequent interruptions scatter our thoughts, weaken our memory, and make us tense and anxious. The more complex the train of thought we're involved in, the greater the impairment the distractions cause.[34]

Carr concludes:

Given our brain's plasticity, we know that our online habits continue to reverberate in the workings of our synapses when we're not online. We can assume that the neural circuits devoted to scanning, skimming, and multitasking are expanding and strengthening, while those used for reading and thinking deeply, with sustained concentration, are weakening or eroding.[35]

34   Nicholas Carr. *The Shallows: What the Internet is Doing to Our Brains* (New York: W.W. Norton, 2010), 132.
35   Ibid., 141

The theological implications of this are serious. The Bible is not a simplistic revelation. Correctly interpreting Scripture and applying its story and promises to our lives requires mature thinking. The church's teaching on sexuality, for example, is rooted in a rich meta-narrative of divine design and human nature. In the disembodied avatar-halls of the Internet, it's not just that these ideas are unpopular, it's that they require a kind of sustained, careful, big-picture thought that the Web actively undermines in its users.

In *The Screwtape Letters*, C.S. Lewis's titular demon advises his protégé to avoid trying to argue with humans. Instead of debating whether such and such religious claim is objectively true, Screwtape urges Wormwood to press jargon on his "patient." "Don't waste time trying to make him think that materialism is true," Screwtape writes. "Make him think it is strong or stark or courageous, that it is the philosophy of the future. That's the sort of thing he cares about."[36] Lewis knew in the 1940s what the Internet age has proved: careful, clear, deep thinking is conducive to Christian faithfulness, but impressionistic, knee-jerk reaction is not.

3. "ANYTHING THAT MAKES ME UNCOMFORTABLE SHOULD NOT EXIST"

Much like how the invention of the automobile not only allowed people's traveling desires but also created and cultivated them, the Internet's curated environment both allows people to remove what they dislike and cultivates a sense that whatever they dislike *ought* to be removed. Among the many dynamics at play with things like "cancel culture," one of them surely is the way Internet technology has lowered our tolerance for things we would like to remove from our screens. The obnoxious email can be deleted, the boring timeline can be refreshed, and the offensive interlocutor can be muted. This perpetual ability to customize what we consume, thanks to the Internet's disembodied nature, trains our consciences in a liturgy of aversion.

36 C.S. Lewis, *The Screwtape Letters*. (New York: HarperCollins, 1942)

Intuitively, we feel that the Internet connects us to people and ideas that we otherwise would not see, and there is indeed truth to this. But it's also true that the form of the Internet actually allows us, in a very powerful sense, to escape anything we encounter. The form of digital technology keeps us at a safe distance from whatever we might object to, even whatever may be for our ultimate good.

In a 2016 essay for *First Things*, Marc Barnes described watching visitors at an art museum. They barely looked at the timeless pieces before them, almost automatically pointing their phone cameras at the art, taking a picture, and then moving on. "The click offers us a way out," he writes. "What does not come naturally can always be aped technologically, and the act of taking a photo mimics the moment of emotion. … We achieve through the lens what we cannot achieve through the heart: a moment in which the object penetrates and changes us according to its own value."[37]

_____

37 "Click Fix," First Things, May 2016 https://www.firstthings.com/article/2016/05/click-fix

Theologically, the ability to curate our reality cripples our capacity to follow the Bible's commands to live counter-intuitively. We're taught to love our enemies, to submit to those in authority, to deny our sinful instincts, to receive a faithful rebuke, to confess our sins, and, perhaps hardest of all, to forgive those who sin against us. None of these practices are celebrated in mainstream online culture, and several of them are considered active evidences of abuse. Why? Because within the moral logic of the Internet, the user is always in control. To follow any of these biblical commands is to concede pride of place in our own story, and the first-person, highly curated, totally customized experience of online life is simply not compatible with this.

CONCLUSION

Expressive individualism's primary channel of personal formation is without a doubt the Internet, which through its nature trains us in these digital liturgies that undermine biblical faithfulness. So what should we do? Should we delete our accounts, cancel our subscriptions, throw out our laptops, and reject the online world? The temptation is strong, and admittedly there are ways that Christians need to seriously rethink automatic acceptance of and participation in these environments.

But we ought to remember that Jesus prayed for his disciples, not that they would be taken out of the world, but protected from the evil one (John 17:15). These digital liturgies do not exist ultimately because of the Internet, but because of the world, which will always express rejection of revealed truth through whatever media are available. The answer cannot be to leave the world, but to participate in the creation of a new one.

Christians will not always successfully resist these digital liturgies, but they will resist them best together. The Internet's most important feature is also its most important weakness. Disembodied "community" does not satisfy the soul, does not cure loneliness, and does not instill a sense of cosmic justice. Only worshipful practices of the local church, through which the Word renews our mind, can do this. As Christians remind each other of the gospel, we will build in one another the capacity for richer joys, deeper identity, and lasting meaning that digital technology promises but never delivers. The permanence of the gospel, revealed in a book, proclaimed by a community, and demonstrated through love, is more than enough ballast for screen-weary souls.

ABOUT THE AUTHOR
Samuel D. James is associate acquisitions editor at Crossway Books, and publishes a regular newsletter called Insights.

Social Media Is Designed to Divide Churches—So What Do We Do?

Clare Morell

Researchers estimate that on average people spend around two and a half hours a day on social media. Compare that with Barna's research that the average Christian spends less than 30 minutes reading the Bible daily, and what you have is a discipleship problem.

With voices on social media getting louder, pastors and churches are finding their voices getting lost in the noise. How should Christians in general and pastors in particular think about discipling amid the proliferation of social media?

Before we answer this question, we first need to understand both the harmful design and the harmful content of social media.

THE DESIGN OF BIG TECH PLATFORMS IS HARMFUL

Social media platforms aren't neutral. They're designed for addiction. Their business model is data extraction, where the service they provide is "free" because you as the user are the product. We pay with our time, attention, and data, which they then sell to advertisers for revenue. To generate more revenue, they need to sell more ads, and to sell more ads, they need to keep us as engaged as possible.

The most effective way they can keep people engaged is by using algorithms. Their algorithms are designed to feed us the content we want to see. The better their algorithms are, the more time we'll stay engaged. It's a deadly combo—their algorithms combined with our sinful tendency to enjoy content that appeals to our flesh. We don't like to grapple with alternative viewpoints. So we don't click on those posts. And so over time the platform doesn't show them to us. What's more, these algorithms drive us into our own bubbles and echo chambers. They incentivize sensational, hyperbolic, and extreme content by promoting sensational, hyperbolic, and extreme content. As a result, our discourse is polarized. And our churches are fracturing.

Finally, the overall design of these platforms encourages the projection and expression of the self out to the universe for the judgment and approval of others. The invention of Facebook's "like" button in 2009 drastically increased this tendency. As these platforms incentivize and encourage self-obsession, we struggle against envy, bitterness, and discontentment in our hearts.

THE CONTENT ON BIG TECH'S PLATFORMS IS HARMFUL

All these negative design features lead to content that traffics in what the Bible calls "desires of the flesh and the desires of the eyes and pride of life" (1 John 2:16).

Let me highlight just a few examples of such content. The first is online pornography and sexually illicit content. Pornography is actively distributed on mainstream social media platforms, like Facebook and Twitter. A recent Wall Street Journal piece highlights how TikTok sends users, including teens, down dangerous rabbit holes of sexual and drug-related content. Instagram has also been found to push drugs on teens. Instagram and TikTok both promote content related to eating disorders and self-harm, particularly to teenage girls. Bizarrely, teen girls are now developing physical tics from watching videos of people with tics on TikTok. Other teens are diagnosing themselves with rare mental disorders due to diagnosis videos on TikTok.

Lastly, social media actively promotes messages and values that are directly opposed to Christian beliefs. Silicon Valley actively manipulates their algorithms to promote various social issues related to gender, sexuality, abortion, and other topics. The rise of transgender influencers and transgender content on social media is deeply disturbing. In her book *Irreversible Damage*, Abigail Shirer explains how the transgender craze affecting our teenage girls is due in large part to the rise of transgender influencers on social media. Most teens who transition didn't start by struggling with the mental illness of body dysmorphia but by watching trans influencers.

HOW CHRISTIANS SHOULD RESPOND

In light of these dangerous realities of social media, how should Christians and churches respond?

1. Consider taking a "social media" sabbatical.

Peter instructs his hearers to pursue "sober mindedness" (1 Peter 1:13, 4:7, 5:8). When it comes to social media, we should be watchful and set clear boundaries. Perhaps we should consider getting off of social media entirely or taking a complete break for different seasons. At the very least, we should make sure that we are not spending more time in our week on social media than in God's Word or with God's people. John Piper once tweeted, "One of the great uses of Twitter and Facebook will be to prove at the Last Day that prayerlessness was not from lack of time."

2. Model Christian social media use for your kids and congregants.

Part of the job of a pastor and a parent is to be a model of godliness. Parents and pastors must model a good use of technology for our children and church members. For parents, this means teaching our kids that living as "strangers and aliens" will mean not having the same access to social media accounts or smart phones that other kids have. For pastors, this will mean avoiding an unhealthy craving for controversy, quarrels about words, dissension, slander, evil suspicions, and constant friction (1 Tim. 6:4–5). It will also mean modeling righteousness, godliness, faith, love, steadfastness, and gentleness (1 Tim. 6:11). Ask a godly friend, or a godly critic, which list best characterizes your use of social media.

3. Prioritize face-to-face interactions over screens

The apostles understood the priority of face-to-face communication (Romans 1:11–12, 2 John 12, 3 John 13). One way we can counteract the culture of expressive individualism on social media is by prioritizing in-person relationships and conversations. There's no better place to do this than in our local churches. As much as possible, we should keep our church small groups, Sunday school classes, Bible studies, and certainly our services in person, rather than online. If we see a member post something online we disagree with, then we should talk to them about it in person rather than online. It's hard work to have conversations with fellow believers that we have strong disagreements with, but it's absolutely necessary. Doing so builds up unity in the church, rather than allowing polarizing online exchanges to divide us.

All of this can be summed up in one word: love. Seek to practice and cultivate self-sacrifice rather than self-expression. Just as the "Son of Man came not to be served, but to serve and give His life as a ransom for many" (Matthew 20:28), we should do the same. Combat the age of expressive individualism and self-promotion through serving others. This life is not about our glory. It's not about us expressing or finding ourselves. So let's give our all to loving and building up his church and glorifying Christ.

A MATTER OF AUTHORITY AND TRUST

At the end of the day, our interaction with social media boils down to bigger questions of authority and trust. Our differing algorithmic experiences have become the dominant source of authority in our lives. And since our algorithms feed us what we want, this is just another way of saying that *we* have become our own final authorities.

To this crisis of authority, the Bible instructs us to look to the authority of parents, pastors, churches, and ultimately God's Word. Are we living according to the authority of our self-selected social media experience, or according to the authority of God's Word? Are we trusting voices on social media that we've never met more than the pastors who baptized us, pray for us, and preach to us? If you're a pastor, are you tweeting for your "audience" on social media at the expense of the congregation God has entrusted to you to steward?

There's no going back to an age before technology. But we must constantly assess our stewardship. As God warned Cain, "Its desire is contrary to you, but you must rule over it" (Gen. 4:7).

ABOUT THE AUTHOR

Clare Morell is a Policy Analyst at the Ethics and Public Policy Center, where she works on EPPC's Big Tech Project. She is also a member of Capitol Hill Baptist Church.

Questions about Gender Should Send Us to Scripture

Tom Schreiner

Many questions have recently been raised about complementarianism. We are keenly aware of the many stories of pastoral and spousal abuse—some of whom are noted complementarians. Such stories make many people wonder if complementarianism is simply a form of power grab, an attempt to hold onto male authority in order to exercise their selfish will.

Cultural questions have been raised as well. Is the complementarian vision merely a product of white western culture—deriving from a patriarchal ethos and an American vision of the good life, entirely sundered from biblical witness?

Or others have suggested the complementarian view solely represents the worldview of the Republican party, constituting a backlash to societal changes in the 1960's. Or as one historian initially proposed, perhaps we have been more influenced by John Wayne than Jesus of Nazareth?

All of the questions posed above are excellent, and we need to be open to critique and revision. I hope none of us would claim that we are perfect in our interpretation or implementation of what the Scriptures teach on the relationship between men and women.

There is always a danger that we have reacted to or imitated the society around us. We are all influenced by culture and should receive any critique that returns us to scriptural witness in good faith. We should listen charitably to brothers and sisters who view things differently—and none of us should be above reforming and nuancing our views.

The matter is complex, however, and egalitarians must also be able to answer the questions that are posed to them. They are not immune to cultural forces either.

The feminism of the 1960's has shaped society in profound and enduring ways—both for good and for ill. The sexual revolution has transformed our culture's conception of what it means to be a man and a woman. This shows up in the acceptance of same-sex marriage and transgender identity, among other things.

Nor can we discount the influence of the mainstream media and major universities, many of which are guided chiefly by leftist ideology. Those who relax the complementarian norm are often celebrated in these spaces as open-minded by a social elite.

In other words, there are social and cultural forces operating on both sides. No one is exempt, and no one inhabits a neutral space when it comes to gender dynamics.

Every argument for every perspective should send us back to the biblical witness. The Word of God still pierces our darkness and can reshape how we think and live. The Bible can and should still be heard, believed, and followed—even though we are all fallible and culturally situated.

Of course, every reading of the biblical text on male-female issues represents an interpretation and is subject to critique. But since there are cultural arguments, forces, and pressures on every side, we must always return to the Scriptures to decipher their meaning—and I believe that meaning can be retrieved.

At the end of the day, it should come down to whoever offers the most plausible and persuasive reading of the biblical texts in question. The complementarian view isn't nullified by saying Trump and Republicanism and the egalitarian reading isn't contradicted by crying out feminism and liberalism.

Yet I worry that in some circles, cultural arguments receive precedence over scriptural ones—as if they alone have the final say on the truth or falsity of a particular biblical interpretation.

EDITOR'S NOTE

This article originally appeared on Christianity Today's website.

ABOUT THE AUTHOR

Thomas R. Schreiner is a Professor of New Testament Interpretation at The Southern Baptist Theological Seminary in Louisville, Kentucky, and the Pastor of Preaching at Clifton Baptist Church. You can find him on Twitter at @DrTomSchreiner.

If You Want to Address LGBTQ, Address Expressive Individualism

Ryan Fullerton

Underneath the flourishing of the LGBTQ movement is a worldview that is shared by almost everyone in our culture. This way of looking at life is often called "expressive individualism." You may not have heard of it before, but as Trevin Wax points out, you have heard it in comments like, "you do you," "be true to yourself," "follow your heart," "find yourself," "be yourself." That's what expressive individualism sounds like in daily life. Can you imagine someone saying to you, "Now it's really important that you *don't* be yourself!" The reason that feels wrong is because expressive individualism is the water we swim in every day.

Furthermore, if you want to help your church know what to make of the LGBTQ movement, as well as their own personal temptations, you'll want to understand the soil out of which it grows. You will want to make sure your people understand this soil as well.

WHAT IS EXPRESSIVE INDIVIDUALISM?

Let's stop for a minute and think about what is behind the "you do you" philosophy of expressive individualism. There are several features. I'll mention three.

First, a person's true self is located in their feelings. I'll give an example. If someone feels like a female even though their birth certificate and biology says they are a male, then many people today would say that makes the person a female. Or if someone feels attracted to people of the same sex, then that's what they are. It's their identity because we believe you are defined by your desires. You are what you feel yourself to be.

Second, the highest goal of expressive individualism is, perhaps unsurprisingly, for you to express yourself. In fact, freedom is getting to express yourself and be yourself.

Third, the ultimate authority in who you ought to be is you—not tradition, or religion, or custom, or government, or biology, just the inner you. If any outside authority gets in the way of your self-expression, then that's oppression. If anyone says you

should be ashamed of who you are or says, "you can't be who you feel you are," then that's abusive.

That's expressive individualism in a nutshell.

THE ROOT OF LGBTQ: EXPRESSIVE INDIVIDUALISM

If you are going to understand the LGBTQ movement, then you need to understand expressive individualism. You see, the letters in the LGBTQ movement are just like floors of a house, and expressive individualism is its foundation.

Let me illustrate. Have you noticed that the LGBTQ list is getting longer? When I was younger, it was just LGBT, then Questioning or Queer was added, and now Intersex and Ally have been added. There's also the "+" because more designations will surely come. You might be tempted to see the letters of LGBTQ as individual flowers in a bouquet—one is a rose, another is a daffodil. You might think each letter is different and all they have in common is that they are *not* traditional straight sexuality. But if you think like that, you might miss that these different sexual identities are actually linked to-gether. They're not flowers in a bouquet, but rather like the honey mushroom in Oregon's Malheur National Forest.

What's the honey mushroom? It's quite possibly the largest liv-ing organism on our planet, cover-ing over three square miles. Now when you see it, you would just see a few little classic mushrooms here and there. But in reality these mushrooms are all interconnect-ed underground. What looks like many mushrooms is actually one.

So it is with the LGBTQ+ movement. The constantly grow-ing letters are actually united by something deeper, something un-derground. They are united by ex-pressive individualism.

What's more, the claims of the LGBTQ+ movement and the claims of Jesus are diametrically opposed. They are set for a head-on collision. Jesus himself says as much:

> If anyone would come after me, let him deny himself and take up his cross and follow me. [35] For whoever would save his life will lose it, but whoever loses his life

for my sake and the gospel's will save it. [36] For what does it profit a man to gain the whole world and forfeit his soul? [37] For what can a man give in return for his soul? [38] For whoever is ashamed of me and of my words in this adul-terous and sinful generation, of him will the Son of Man also be ashamed when he comes in the glory of his Father with the holy angels. (Mk 8:34–38)

These words are decidedly *not* the air we breathe. These are counter cultural words from the King of Kings and Lord of Lords.

HOW DO WE RESPOND TO LGBTQ?

So with the contrast and the clash clearly in our minds, how should pastors respond to the LGBTQ+ movement?

1. Point to the underground issue.

Pastors should start by helping their churches see the honey mush-room—the whole underground system—out of which individual mushrooms grow: expressive indi-vidualism. If we wanted to kill the honey mushroom, we wouldn't get very far simply by picking off individual mushrooms that emerged on the surface. We would need to get underground and destroy the larger system.

Insofar as expressive individualism remains the default worldview of our church members, they will continue to feel an intuitive pull towards creating moral space for LGBTQ+ affirmation. They'll see the biblical prooftexts that tell them sexual immorality is wrong, but their moral intuitions will *feel* otherwise. Something inside of them will keep saying, "Really? Do we have to say this is wrong?"

Therefore, show your people the relationship between the LGBTQ+ movement and expressive individualism. Doing so will help them recognize the source of that inner voice. It will address those deeper intuitions and help them to avoid being conformed to the pattern of this world and to be transformed by the renewing of their minds. It will also help them avoid self-righteous condemnation.

2. Teach the basics of what it means to follow Jesus.

Of course, you can't just point to the underground root system. You have to replace it with something else. We do this by pointing to passages like Mark 8:34-38 again and again and reminding them of the basic call of Christian repentance and discipleship. It's a call that envelopes every area of our lives, including our sexuality and identity.

First, we're called to deny ourselves—or, to put it another way, to flee sin. Jesus isn't saying you should deny your own existence, to pretend you don't exist, or to commit mental suicide. Denying yourself doesn't lead to non-existence; it leads to a new way of living which Jesus sums up as following him. Denying yourself also doesn't mean you must deny all your desires for goodness and happiness. Jesus is not calling his people to be stoics who turn off their emotions and block out their desires. No, this whole passage speaks to those who don't want to lose their lives, to people who want to keep their souls, and who do not want to feel the shame of Jesus being ashamed of them. So what self-denial is Jesus talking about? He's talking about our deep personal desires for sin. He wants us to put away all sinful ways of finding joy in life, all earthly hopes of enjoying the good life. He wants us to deny all sinful impulses, temptations, and desires and instead to follow Jesus. To deny yourself is to flee your own desires for sin so you can follow the Savior.

Second, we're called to our take up our cross—or, to put it another way, to embrace the shame that comes with following Jesus. Many people talk about cross-bearing in ways that have very little to do with Jesus and his actual cross. They get a sore back and they say, "This is my Cross to bear." That's not the central idea here. When Jesus took up the cross he was embracing public shame (Hebrews 12:2).

Think of the things that make you ashamed. No one wants to be naked in public, but on the cross Jesus was splayed out naked in public with no ability to cover himself. He did not die dressed in style; he died shamefully covered in blood, spit, and tattered flesh. None of us want people to see us when we're sniffling and sneezing and feeling terrible. Jesus died in public panting for breath. None of us like to have a bad reputation for something we haven't done. We don't want to be "slut-shamed" or called a racist. But Jesus, the righteous man, hung naked on a cross like a common criminal. The godliest man the world has ever known was hung on a cross for being a blasphemer. He was shamed.

To follow Christ, you and I are called to embrace a life of being shamed. We follow the one who had shame heaped upon him, but we are not ashamed of him. His death on the cross for us is precious to us. So even though the world shames us for being associated with such a rigid, restrictive God and all his backward ideas, we embrace that shame and take up our cross to follow him.

Third and finally, we follow him. Notice that believers don't look inward to find their marching orders. Everything we do is for him, even if it costs us everything. Did you hear him call us to be unashamed of him and his words? We are following the one who serves others, washes feet, submits to God's natural world and God's biblical commands. If believers have an orientation, it's not inward but outward and toward Christ. We follow him.

Christian discipleship doesn't say "you do you"; it says "no, you follow me." This is the most merciful call in the world. Our own choices lead us to all kinds of misery, but merciful Jesus calls us to follow him, the most loving, holy, human, divine, person who ever lived. What compassionate grace!

3. We should compassionately expose LGBTQ sins.

We live in a world where many believe that LGBTQ lifestyles will bring them satisfaction. In fact, all LGBTQ sexual activity goes painfully against the grain of nature. This is one of the central truths the Bible brings up specifically when it deals with homosexual and transgender sins. Speaking of God's wrath on humanity, Paul says,

God gave them up to dishonorable passions. For their women exchanged natural relations for those that are contrary to nature; and the men likewise gave up natural relations with women and were consumed with passion for one another, men committing shameless acts with men and receiving in themselves the due penalty for their error. (Rom 1:26)

Notice Paul called sexual relations between a man and a woman natural, while lesbian and homosexual passions unnatural (cf Jude 7). Like all things that go against the grain of nature, they bring their own consequences in this life, the "due penalty" in themselves for their error. Elsewhere, when Paul speaks of men looking like men and women looking like women, he brings up nature again, "Does not nature itself teach you that if a man wears long hair it is a disgrace for him, but if a woman has long hair, it is her glory?" (1 Co 11:14–15)

It's interesting when issues of sexual identity and gender identity come up in the Bible, nature is invoked. We know instinctively that men should dress and identify as men. We know instinctively that a man and a woman's genitals fit together. I'm going to be graphic for a moment, but the reason I'm doing this is that when we talk about LGBTQ issues we often do so under the vague umbrella of love, and so we neglect to spell out what is actually going on in nature. When a man has anal intercourse with a man, it rips, it tears, it bleeds. It increases the chance of disease, and it makes your bum leak. When a man and a woman come together in vaginal intercourse, it is safe, naturally lubricated, and life creating. When a man and a man come together, the seed of life that comes out of a man is swallowed up in the bowels of defecation and death (Budziszewski, *What We Can't Not No*). It's not a natural action or desire. Furthermore, the results of these unnatural desires are severe. The Vanderbilt University Medical Center reports, "Men who have sex with men and gay men are at increased risk for certain types of chronic diseases, cancers, and mental health problems." Gay men are at risk for HIV, HPV, Drug Abuse, Depression and Anxiety, Body Image Issues like anorexia, and bulimia. Transgender people are also susceptible to these same diseases, and their suicide rates are very high as well (Sharon James, *Gender Ideology*).

Someone could say that all the depression, the drug abuse, and the body image issues are because preachers like me keep telling people that these desires are unnatural. That would be one explanation. The other would be that when you go against nature there are predictable results. If you fill your lungs with carbon dioxide instead of oxygen there will be some predictable results. If you eat gravel for breakfast instead of granola there will be some predictable results (Budziszewski, *The Meaning of Sex*). And if you use your body unnaturally then there will be some predictable results.

We are afraid to speak like this because we fear it lacks compassion. But isn't it the height of compassion to share these truths with the world? We lovingly warn people about cigarettes and lung cancer but not about all the disease and depression that goes with sexual sin. Perhaps people will hear us and start to see that going down unnatural and harmful ways will hurt them. Perhaps they will see our warnings as a mercy, as a compassionate call from the God of creation who said, "Deny yourself, take up your Cross, and follow me." We should compassionately talk about LGBTQ issues as the unnatural sins they are, and we should invite unbelievers (and Christians who struggle) into the joy of denying self and following Jesus.

4. We should wisely reject LGBTQ identity.

Some Christians today say gay people should embrace a traditional Christian sexual ethic while at the same time refusing to reject a gay identity. These men and women would agree with the Bible that sexual activity should occur only within a heterosexual marriage. So far so good. However, they'd also think it's entirely acceptable for Christians who feel gay to identify as such. They argue that how you feel oriented inside defines your identity. I have two responses.

First, the inclination to identify your real self with your internal desires is shaped more by expressive individualism than by biblical faith. Labeling your ultimate identity by your sexual desires is not the way the Bible speaks about us.

Pastors, we should encourage our people to think about themselves the way the Bible encourages us to think about our identities.

Second, it strikes me as odd that we don't deal with any of sin like this. For example, I've struggled with anger as a Christian. Should I self-identify as an angry Christian? One preacher pointed out that we would not walk around and say something like, "I'm a racist. I mean don't get me wrong, I don't practice racism, but in terms of my orientation, I prefer the company of white people. I feel white culture is better." It sucks the wind out of me to say that.

"I'm a gay Christian" should sound the same to us. As Christians, our ultimate identity comes through who God made us (we are his creatures), who we are in Christ (we are new creatures in Christ), and the roles God gives us (as parents, children, and brothers and sisters in the Church). Real Christians can be tempted by homosexual desires and transgender confusion. They can feel them deep inside their bones. And yet, no Christian ought to label themselves with those temptations. Our primary identity is that we are in Christ. We come to him, we follow him, and we are not ashamed of him.

5. We should lovingly oppose LGBTQ oppression.

It's often easy to see oppression in the past. It's easy looking back and to see the evil of American slavery. It's also easy to see oppression far away. The reports that come out of North Korea remind us that we have many brothers and sisters who are imprisoned and being tortured in our time.

It's harder to see oppression up close. But make no mistake: the LGBTQ agenda is deeply oppressive. For example, many Christians have come to the conviction that we should not call someone by their preferred pronouns. To call a "she" a "he" or a "he" a "she" breaks the ninth commandment: do not bear false witness. But a Christian in New York today could be fined $250,000 for not using someone's preferred pronouns. In 2017, an Ohio couple lost custody of their own child when they refused to help them transition to the opposite sex.

Across America, women are losing in women's sports as mediocre men declare themselves women and use their superior masculine speed, athleticism, and strength to dominate. I suppose losing a gold medal is not oppression, but losing athletic scholarships to men means fewer women who will go to college for free.

In Canada, a law (Bill C-4) was recently passed that makes conversion therapy illegal. What is "conversion therapy"? Well, the law states that "conversion therapy means a practice, treatment or service designed to change a person's sexual orientation to heterosexual; change a person's gender expression so that it conforms to the sex assigned to the person at birth; or repress or reduce non-heterosexual attraction or sexual behavior." Put simply, that makes it illegal to offer the hope of the gospel to same-sex attracted people.

Will this mean that a Christian preacher or Christian counselor who tries to help people reject unnatural desires will be fined or imprisoned? That remains to be seen. But we should be vocal like Jesus against this kind of evil. And yet, I want you to realize something: resisting this oppression will probably not happen in some dramatic speech, it will come when you say no to the pride pin they're handing out at work, or refuse to put your pronouns on your name-tag because you won't play that game. Yes, we must personally love LGBTQ people. More on that below. But I want to be clear that speaking truth about public issues so that people are not bankrupted, robbed of scholarships, or imprisoned for speaking the truth—that's loving and compassionate, too.

6. We should eagerly love LGBTQ people with the gospel.

As Christians, we understand that all people, no matter how sinful their desires may be, are made in the image of God. On top of that, we follow a Savior who drew near to all sorts of sinful people. He was a friend of sinners. Our LGBTQ friends are sinners—like all of us—so we should show kindness to them.

We should have them into our homes, invite them to our churches, and read the Bible with them. We should find ways to show mercy to those suffering from AIDS, depression, and drug abuse. My old pastor in Toronto used to walk into an area of town where many gay men lived and express to them how much he longed for them to visit his church. We need more of that. Many of you will know the story of Rosaria Butterfield who was a lesbian University professor who was befriended by a pastor and his wife and over time led to the Lord. More of that, please!

Now, I know that in many situations your compassionate love and sharing of the good news will not be met with open arms. Calling people to repentance can be called abusive these days. Speaking about God's standards can be called oppressive. Telling people that their only hope is in the cross of Christ has always seemed foolish to the world. But the world is terribly deceived. The world thinks cutting off a transgendered child's genitals may be liberating. No, that's abuse. The world may not love us, but we must love them even if they slander and misunderstand us. But if you are maligned, reviled, or even persecuted, then you are in good company. They did that to Jesus and the prophets. Our job is not to control people's reactions to us, our job is to show the love of Christ to sinners.

ABOUT THE AUTHOR

Ryan Fullerton is the senior pastor at Immanuel Baptist Church in Louisville, Kentucky. You can find him on Twitter at @RyanFullerton. Church Stories.

Expressive Individualism, Embodied Telos, and How to Be an Anti-Winfrey

Andrew Walker

Appearing on her Apple TV+ series in April 2021, super-celebrity Oprah Winfrey interviewed popular actress "Elliot" Page, formerly Ellen Page. Page made headlines in December 2020 when she announced that she was transgender. Appearing on the cover of *TIME Magazine*, Page was heralded worldwide for her bravery. But on screen with Winfrey, Page exuded awkward discomfort, even sorrow.

Winfrey began the segment with a monologue:

> Before we begin I want to say to you and to our viewers all over the Apple world and on Apple TV+ that my hope is that this conversation can serve as an invitation for all of us to understand, for all of us to appreciate, and for all

of us to know that inside ourselves that every human born to the planet wants the same thing and that is to be accepted to be loved and to live in health and safety as our authentic selves. And I really want to honor and celebrate your courage, Elliot, for sharing your truth on social media, then, on the cover of *TIME Magazine*, and now in this conversation with me, so I honor that."

Pastor, your job is to love the Ellens or Elliots who show up in your church far more than Winfrey does. Winfrey's honor and celebration is a fake honor and celebration. It has nothing to do with honoring and celebrating who God created her to be. Just as the apostle John tells us that we're surrounded by antichrists (1 John 4:19), then, you're to be an anti-Winfrey—for love's sake. Your job is to honor and celebrate the embodied persons that God created every man and woman to be, and to teach your congregation to do the same.

EXPRESSIVE INDIVIDUALISM AND OUR EMBODIED TELOS

Winfrey is a pastor in the church of expressive individualism. And her statement offers a near-perfect example of how expressive individualism denies that a person's biological sex determines his or her embodied telos.

I know I sound like an ethics professor when I talk that way. So let me break it down.

Nearly everyone in history has understood—and the Bible teaches—that our bodies come in two sexually complementary forms, and that those differently formed bodies are part of what constitute who we are and the purpose of our lives. Our reproductive design exhibits purposes essential to the nature of being immutably "male" or "female." In other words, our biologically-and-sexually-distinct bodies possess a "telos"—an *end*, *goal*, or *purpose*.

Therefore, Christian discipleship must account for our embodied telos—who God means for us to be as biological men and women, his purpose in those realities, and how those wonderful realities are significant in the grand project of following Christ together in the fellowship of his church. The fact that we've been creating male and female—and why these realities are significant—is part of discipleship 101. Yet this embodied telos is exactly what expressive individualism rejects.

"Expressive individualism" is a way of thinking or a worldview whereby individuals believe their dignity and personhood depend on casting off any and all relationships and traditions—including religion—that get in the way of their deepest and most authentic selves. Expressive individualism posits that our flourishing depends on self-actualization—building our identities on our own perceptions, desires, and choices. It argues that our identities are based not on "nature" but on what one *wants* or *chooses* or *feels*. It is necessarily appetitive. And, along the way, it denies any telos exists for what it means to be male or female. Our biological structures pose no normative authority or say whatsoever in determining who we are or

the purpose of our biological sex. We are merely blank canvases of raw biological material on which to paint the portrait of whomever you will yourself to be.

A BETTER VIEW OF THE BODY

So go back to Winfrey's statement: "inside...every human... wants the same thing...to be accepted...as our authentic selves." Notice, there is no immutable relationship between the body's authority and the self's understanding of its identity. Rather, she offers a form of Gnosticism, where the true "self" is severed from the body. Philosopher Robert P. George notes how, for the pop-Gnosticism of transgenderism, "the body serves as the pleasure of the conscious self, to which it is subject, and so mutilations and other procedures pose no inherent moral problem."

Winfrey depicts herself as in no position to question the coherence of Page's claim about herself. She can only defer to the "lived experience" of Page. To do otherwise would be to commit the principal blasphemy law of the age of expressive individualism.

But pastors, as an anti-Winfrey, you must hold out a simultaneously more negative and positive vision of the self. You should help your congregation be suspicious of the fallen self, it's impulses and desires. But you should also help them recognize that when God created the male and female bodies, he said, "It is very good." Christianity doesn't deny the body. It affirms the body—sexuality and all—and God's good purposes for it.

A BETTER VIEW OF LIBERTY

Pastors must also hold out a better and more biblical view of liberty. A biblical definition of liberty treats it as the freedom and ability to do what one *ought*. Once you've been set free by the gospel, you're no longer enslaved to sin and obeying its desires, you're free by God's Spirit to pursue his righteousness. Knowing the truth sets us free, says Jesus.

Notice that in the biblical definition, there is a presumed rationale for why political civil rights are afforded to individuals: for individuals to live according to the truth of their nature. This speaks to the authority and prescriptivity that comes within a teleological worldview.

Individual expressionism, however, redefines liberty merely as license. This redefinition misunderstands human nature. It denies any fixed concept of human nature. It forfeits any sort of bounded notion of teleology or purpose. Not surprisingly, these misunderstandings and denials make their way deep into the heat of American culture and American jurisprudence, as when Anthony Kennedy defined liberty as "the right to define one's own concept of existence, of meaning, of the universe, and of the mystery of human life" in order to justify abortion. His expressive individualism, in other words, yielded a liberty that leads to murder and death.

In short, expressive individualism undermines an embodied telos, which ultimately yields the elimination of the self through abortion as well as the redefinition of the self through "gender transitions."

THE BIBLE PLACES OUR TELOS INSIDE OF CREATION

Back to your job description, pastor. Your job is to teach the Bible, and the Bible offers the antidote to expressive individualism's universal acid. Expressive individualism prizes autonomy above all things, attempting to free us even from the laws of creation. It rebels from something even as basic as the fact that we are of creation. The Bible, however, places the human person suitably inside of a good creation and the providential ordering of a loving God. And inside of that creation and in God's revealed purposes in it we discover crucial elements of our teleology.

Alasdair MacIntyre has observed, "Every craft is informed by some conception of a finally perfected work which serves as the shared telos of that craft. And what are actually produced as the best judgments or actions or objects so far are judged so because they stand in some determinate relationship to that telos, which furnishes them with their final cause." As Christians, we should measure human excellence and Christian discipleship (MacIntyre's idea of the "craft") by its conformity to God as the ultimate telos, and God's sovereignty over our nature as the penultimate telos.

Scripture portrays us as gendered image-bearers. Genesis 1 and 2 presents Adam and Eve as teleological creatures placed inside of a teleological order. He gives them a habitable world, and he commissions them to be fruitful and multiply and to fill the earth. Our purpose for existing, then, must somehow be bound up in fulfilling this commission, which necessarily requires two different bodily kinds. The Bible's first pages, in other words, offers us an enchanted, teleological order directed by God's providence.

God does not create by chaos. There is no capriciousness in his ordering of creation. He creates us to act for certain ends. As Matthew Levering observes, "God creates human beings so that they are naturally ordered to preserve the good of their human existence."

PASTOR, YOU GET TO OFFER WHAT'S TRULY GOOD

The political rhetoric of our present moment makes pastors and Christians out to be the bad guys. And, if we're honest, sometimes this rhetoric can get inside our heads. "Am I being intolerant? Am I denying people love and joy and the good life?" Church members, at least, can wonder this.

My goal, then, is to hearten you, pastor. You're offering your church and the non-Christians they bring with them what's truly good. And I don't just mean the good of God and the gospel—the greatest goods. I mean the good that comes with the Bible's teaching about manhood and womanhood and our embodied telos.

To know what is "good" requires a true knowledge of a thing's nature, of what completes it. To experience goodness, then, requires knowing ourselves as image-bearers of God and accepting our being as created by God and living accordingly. No violation of a creature's nature can ever be "good."

Furthermore, knowing the ends of a particular thing allows us to formulate rules of moral action, rules that protect the development and realization of our created purpose. Those rules, in other words, are for our good, and we will experience the good that God intends for us as creatures by obeying those rules.

Expressive individualism, however, offers just the opposite: self-destruction. By denying our God-given teleology, we have created a new class of victims: those known online as "De-Transitioners"—individuals who underwent some degree of "transition" and found no improvement to their underlying psychological pathology.

Yet the ravages of self-destruction extend much farther than these individuals. One Oxford University philosopher, Jacqueline A. Laing, decries this modern idea of liberty that "prides itself on having secured certain rights and freedoms—to destroy one's self, one's offspring, and collectively to destroy one's culture."

This destruction, in short, is what the Winfreys and all the reigning philosophies of this age, backed by the principalities and powers, honor and celebrate as they laud Elliot Page's "courageous" decision. Do you risk being the bad guy in this story, pastor? Yes, indeed.

The duty of pastors in an age of expressive individualism is to re-enchant the beauty and wonder of the human person within the drama of a created order. Help your congregation—the teens, the singles, the young marrieds, the elderly—to rejoice at the idea of creaturely limitation and God's good purposes in those limitations. Help them to proclaim what David says in Psalm 100: "Know that the Lord, he is God! It is he who made us, and we are his; we are his people, and the sheep of his pasture."

ABOUT THE AUTHOR

Andrew T. Walker serves as Associate Professor of Christian Ethics at The Southern Baptist Theological Seminary and is a Fellow with The Ethics and Public Policy Center.

Are You Principled or Just a Contentious Jerk?

Paul Martin

The apostle Paul says "an overseer must be...not quarrelsome" (1 Tim. 3:2–3). Yet in my experience, quarrelsome people often hide behind the excuse, "I'm just principled" or "I'm standing up for the truth when no one else will."

It's not a completely unreasonable point. Many people seem to confuse having an opinion with being quarrelsome, hostile, and aggressive. But that's not right.

So how do you know if you're principled or just a contentious jerk?

My old Webster's Dictionary defines quarrelsome as "apt or disposed to find fault; contentious." Paul described how to not be contentious this way: "Let all **bitterness** and **wrath** and **anger** and **clamor** and **slander** be put away from you, along with all **malice**" (Eph. 4:31).

In other words, if you're prone to debate, to sow discord, or to cause strife, then you are a contentious, quarrelsome person. If you are hungry for a good online fight or more committed to winning an argument than winning over an opponent, then you are a quarrelsome person.

To be sure, you might be principled, too. Being principled doesn't mean you're exempt from the possibility of being quarrelsome. A principled person can indeed be quarrelsome in a way that disqualifies him from the office of elder.

If that's you, you need to repent today.

SIX CHARACTERISTICS OF A QUARRELSOME PERSON

Paul makes this perfectly clear as he details the six sins that must be violently killed if you claim to be a follower of Jesus. These six sins create a quarrelsome person.

1. Take off all bitterness.

A bitter person is sour, crabby, disagreeable, and often trying to find wrong in others. He lives with a suspicious eye, never taking anyone at face value. He is resentful and seldom happy with anyone (except himself).

If you find yourself consumed with how others have offended you, then you are a bitter person. If you've got a pristine Record of Wrongs Done Against Me and you use it to fight every debate you're in, then you are a bitter person.

Friend, this is not good. Dig out the bitterness and throw it in the ditch where it belongs.

2. Take off all wrath.

Paul uses the word "wrath" here to describe those explosions of anger when you lose control, when you find yourself boiling over with rage. There's never an excuse for this kind of behavior in a Christian. It's never acceptable. It's always a sin. It must be mortified, not mollified.

3. Take off all anger.

Unlike "wrath," the anger the Apostle is talking about here is that settled internal disposition or state of mind where a person is just mad about everything and everyone. If you find yourself thinking no one can do right in your eyes, then you are not only arrogant, you're an angry man. Put it to death, brother!

4. Take off all clamor.

We do not use the word clamor a lot, but think of it as an ALL CAPS screed on your socials. Clamor is basically uncontrolled screaming at another person, whether that other person is a spouse in your home or a political foe on the street corner. Did Jesus scream at his enemies? No, and neither should we.

5. Take off all slander.

There are many accusations of slander floating around the blogosphere, but foundationally the word means speaking evil of another. When you use words—spoken or typed—to tear down another, to call them names, to mock them (Prov. 17:5), or to damage their reputation, then you have slandered. In doing so, you have identified much more closely with Satan than any Christian ever should.

6. Take off malice.

Ever found yourself walking away from a difficult conversation imagining all the things you *could* have said, or all the things you *will* say if the opportunity presents itself again? That is called malice. It involves making wicked and evil plans or plotting cruel revenge. Such scheming, too, must stop. Kill this sin or it will kill you.

When you put these six nouns together, you get a detailed description of a contentious person. This person lives with an internal state of mind on high alert for the next scuffle they can start or jump in to.

If a person is bitter and angry, if he is plotting the takedown of other believers, if he is constantly shouting in person or through his keyboard, then he is *quarrelsome*. It doesn't matter if the content of what he says is *right*. It doesn't matter if he's a pastor. You can be right, but malicious. You can say true things while slandering someone. Malice, slander, clamor, anger, wrath, and bitterness are *sins*. And no matter what or who you're fighting against, such sins have no place in the Christian life. Zero.

You must remove these behaviors entirely.

Did you see the word "all" in Ephesians 4:31? "Let **all** bitterness and wrath and anger and clamor and slander be put away from you, along with **all** malice."

All of it! Not *some* of it! Not, *most* of it! All of it. There is no room for them. Not in your church. Not in you.

In fact, these particular sins grieve God the Holy Spirit. Consider the previous verse: "And do not **grieve** the Holy Spirit of God, by whom you were sealed for the day of redemption" (4:30).

The Holy Spirit loves you, Christian, and the Holy Spirit loves your brother, too. When you are contentious with your brother, you wound the heart of God: "But if you bite and devour one another, watch out that you are not consumed by one another. But I say, walk by the Spirit, and you will not gratify the desires of the flesh" (Galatians 5:15–16).

O Contentious Man, you are of the flesh! You are living for yourself!

CONCLUSION

There's a way to say the right thing in the wrong way—to be principled and quarrelsome. Just as there's a way to say the wrong thing in the right way. I am calling on you to say the right things in the right way. To set your sights on honest unity instead of bludgeoned conformity.

As Peter writes, "Finally, all of you, have unity of mind, sympathy, brotherly love, a tender heart, and a humble mind" (1 Peter 3:8).

One of the Dutch versions translated this, "All of you, be friendly with one another..."

They might have been on to something.

ABOUT THE AUTHOR

Paul Martin is a pastor of Grace Fellowship Church in Toronto, Ontario.

Are you Contending for the Truth or Quarrelsome?

Paul Alexander

To be quarrelsome is to be over-eager to fight, whether verbally, physically, or legally. Paul said that neither elders (1 Tim 1:6-7; 3:3; 2 Ti 2:23) nor congregations (Ti 3:2, 9; James 4:1-2) are to be quick to "throw down". Yet Scripture commands to contend for the faith (Jude 3). So how do we tell the difference between fighting the good fight and just being an Argumentative Alex? Here are five quick questions to see if we're quarrelsome.

1. *Are we quick to fight for our rights, whether material or political? (Js 4:1; Titus 3:2).* In Js 4, the coveting that leads to quarreling always starts with a comparison of self to others, where self seems to get the short end of the stick. Contentment in Christ quells that kind of quarrel. This goes politically as well (Titus 3:1-2). Contentment with political disappointments, sustained by a firm faith in God's providence over politics, goes a long way to quelling a quarrelsome heart.

2. *Are we fighting over issues of conviction or conscience?* Is this an essential doctrine like the divinity of Jesus, or substitutionary atonement? Or is this something we can disagree about with others yet still trust and worship Jesus together? Consult Andy Naselli's little book *Conscience:*

What It Is, How to Train it, and Loving Those Who Differ. This will help us know which battles we can (and maybe should) lose.

3. *Are we too excited about speculative theology?* If so, it'll be easy to get under our skin when people disagree with our "creative" interpretations of obscure passages (1 Ti 3:2; Ti 3:2; Dt 29:29). Think about the issue in your context that's most upsetting to you. Is the gospel itself really what's at stake in that disagreement?

4. *Are we quick to fight for our ministry ambitions?* Sometimes in pastoral ministry we want to do good things that are not actually ours to do. David wanted to build God a temple, and God said "not yet, and not you." Pastor, your church cannot be quiet until your own heart is content … not complacent, just content.

5. *Do you respond to quarreling with kindness, or do you to take immediate offense?* After warning us to avoid quarreling in Titus 3:2, Paul says in the next verse "For we ourselves were once foolish, disobedient, led astray, slaves to various passions and pleasures, passing our days in malice and envy, hated by others and hating one another." Being quarrelsome was the foolish mentality of our pre-Christian lives—that's the way we *used* to be. The implication is that we can and should respond to quarrelsomeness from others with the compassion we ourselves have received in the kindness of the gospel.

In fact, that's where Paul goes next in Ti 3:4–8—the gospel of salvation by God's mercy to us in Christ, apart from our works, through the Spirit's regeneration and renewal of our hearts. God's goodness and kindness to us in Jesus—contrary to our previous quarrels against him!—motivates and empowers our own compassion for those who are still quarrelsome toward us. Paul summarizes the gospel here in Titus 3 and tells Titus "insist on these things" (Ti 3:4–8). Are *those* the things *you* are insisting on? Or are you just being quarrelsome?

ABOUT THE AUTHOR

Paul Alexander is the Pastor of Grace Covenant Baptist Church in Elgin, Illinois.

What Does Proverbs Teach about Being Quarrelsome?

Mark Redfern

Paul says an elder must not be quarrelsome (1 Tim. 3:2-3). What can we learn from the book of Proverbs about what it means to be quarrelsome?

WHAT IS QUARRELSOMENESS IN PROVERBS?

A brief survey of the Proverbs offers a helpful summary of "quarrelsomeness." It is a form of "strife"— relational conflict, disagreement, tension, and verbal fighting between individuals (Prov. 17:14; 20:3). Proverbs implicates both genders in this tendency. The "quarrelsome wife" (Prov. 19:13; 21:9, 19; 25:24; 27:14) and the "quarrelsome man" (Prov. 20:3; 26:21) are both identified.

What form does this "relational conflict" take? Quarreling is when a conversation begins to ramp up in intensity: "The beginning of strife is like letting out water, so quit before the quarrel breaks out" (Prov. 17:14). Quarreling is what happens when people enjoy the "drama" of a verbal joust rather than working patiently toward solutions (Prov. 18:18, 26:21).

Quarreling occurs when people are entrenched in their positions and unwilling to give an inch to others (Prov. 18:19). It is the mark of a fool (Prov. 20:3).

WHERE DOES QUARRELSOMENESS COME FROM?

In Proverbs, quarrelsomeness tends to reside among those who have strong opinions. Proverbs calls such people "powerful contenders" (Prov. 18:18). These people are "unyielding" (Prov. 18:19). They have very few unarticulated thoughts. They are easily triggered by what others say. They have a perspective that they want others to embrace, and they are willing to "go to the mat" over it. These are not wholesome arguments, marked by charity, listening, humility, clarifying questions, and genuine inquisitiveness. Rather, they're fruit of a person who feels "alive" when they engage in heated, confrontational dialogue with other image-bearers.

Also, Proverbs presents quarrels as arising out of personal offense (Prov. 18:19). Someone says something they don't like and so they respond. We take it upon ourselves to inform the person of our opinion, to correct their position, or to attack their person. If we feel slighted or insulted, we are pulled toward quarreling.

HOW IS QUARRELSOMENESS ADDRESSED?

If we find ourselves in the midst of a quarrel, Proverbs offers simple counsel: *stop it.* Just "quit" (Prov. 17:14). To those who are tempted to engage in a quarrel, we are told quite directly: *don't.* If we do, we'll get bit (Prov. 26:17). We must "keep aloof" from such things (Prov. 20:3) and if necessary drive such behavior out of our midst (Prov. 22:10). "For lack of wood the fire goes out, and where this is no whisperer, quarreling ceases" (Prov. 26:20).

Quarreling, like a fire, feeds on fresh wood. If the wise keep their mouths shut around foolish quarrelers and resolve to maintain unarticulated opinions on any number of disputable matters, they will find themselves participating in far fewer fights. After all, the wise find quarrelsomeness to be a great annoyance (Prov. 19:13; 27:15). It is exhausting and not at all life-giving. They would rather live in a desert (Prov. 21:19) or on the corner of a housetop (Prov. 21:9) than be involved in another senseless argument.

What about you? Do you find your heart exposed by these Proverbs? If so, feel free to get in on this rebuke if the shoe fits, and let's resolve to walk in the ways of the wise. I see the seeds of this in my own life and am eager not to fertilize them lest I reap a bumper crop in the flesh.

ABOUT THE AUTHOR

Mark Redfern is a pastor of Heritage Baptist Church in Owensboro, KY.

What Does Paul Mean by "Quarrelsome"?

Will McKinney

Brother, whether you're an elder or an aspiring elder, Scripture calls you to live a life characterized by Christlike humility. Paul instructs Timothy, "And the Lord's servant must not be quarrelsome but kind to everyone, able to teach, patiently enduring evil" (2 Timothy 2:24; cf 1 Tim 3:3). Let's focus briefly on the requirement to "not be quarrelsome."

What does Paul have in mind with that word "quarrelsome"?

First of all, the word here translated as "not quarrelsome" is ἄμαχος (amachos), translated by BDAG as "peaceable." This word is also found in Titus 3:2, where Paul tells Titus "to malign no one, to be *uncontentious*, gentle, showing every consideration for all men" (NASB). The other characteristics in Titus 3:2 surrounding the word "uncontentious" help us to understand what this word means. It is to speak favorably of others, to be Christ-like, humble, and gentle (Matt. 11:29). The tenderness and care Christ shows toward the bruised reed and smoldering wick must also be evident in the words of his under shepherds.

To be uncontentious means to avoid fighting. As 2 Timothy 2:23 says, "Have nothing to do with foolish, ignorant controversies; you know that they breed *quarrels* (μάχας)." Similarly, in Titus 3:9, "But avoid foolish controversies and genealogies and strife and *disputes* (μάχας) about the Law, for they are unprofitable and worthless." These controversies result in quarrels. So, if we want to avoid fighting and quarrels then we must stay away from the controversies described in these verses.

Simply put, a quarrelsome man argues about foolish controversies. He doesn't have the sense to realize that what he is talking about will not be profitable. He continues to tread into conversation topics that breed division, not unity. He focuses on secondary or tertiary issues of the faith in an argumentative fashion; he frequently wants to argue and discuss these things.

At times, it's important to discuss controversial or challenging topics. How a man addresses these topics will show his character. When they're discussed, they should be done while showing consideration for others (Titus 3:2).

So ask yourself: Do you discuss these issues with empathy while attempting to understand the other person's position? In difficult conversations, are you a peacemaker or a pugilist? Do you think that you're the expert that others need? Do you think that qualifies you to teach and correct them? Do you come to conversations wanting to be listened to, or do you strive to be a good listener?

In summary, a quarrelsome, contentious person wants to argue and fight the right issues, but they do so usually at the wrong time and in the wrong way. Does this describe you? Discuss these questions with someone who knows you well, like an elder in your church.

May the Lord help us as we see our sin and ask him to conform us more closely into the image of the Chief Shepherd who is gentle and lowly.

ABOUT THE AUTHOR
Will McKinney is a Pastor-teacher at IECD

How Do We Recognize Quarrelsome People?

Nathan Loudin

For a season I came home from every deacons meeting frustrated and exhausted. I was serving as interim pastor at an international church and our deacons were functioning as elders. One of our deacons had quarreled with the previous pastor and it persisted under my leadership. I came to dread being together. Something had to change.

Eventually, we presented one of the most prominent men in our church with a letter asking him to peacefully step down. His first reaction, of course, was resistance. "God and this church made me a deacon and I'm not stepping down." We were prepared to bring his office before the church if he refused. By God's grace, he chose a more peaceful path.

That brings up a question: can we actually discern when a brother or sister is quarrelsome? We can. In fact, the Bible expects us to recognize quarrelsome people.

CHRISTIANS SHOULD RECOGNIZE QUARRELSOME PEOPLE

More than merely describing a *debate* or a *disagreement* itself as a quarrel, the Bible instructs the church to discern when a *person* is quarrelsome. Consider the qualification of elders as. An elder should not *"be … quarrelsome"* (1 Tim 3:3).

So Paul means you must *exist* in certain ways in order to serve as an elder. "Not quarrelsome" should describe *your being*.

Because of this, a quarreler can really be only discerned over time. One quarrelsome exchange may require forgiveness and reconciliation. Another may make you raise your eyebrows about someone serving as an elder. But a few impassioned debates does not a quarreler make.

So how can we tell? Here are a few ways quarrelsome character manifests itself.

1. COIN FLIPS DON'T STOP QUARRELERS | PROVERBS 18:18

If you were to seek to resolve a decision with a fair, impartial method, don't expect a quarreler to accept the resolution. Should our team jersey be blue or red? That is an amoral decision that could be solved by flipping a coin. But a quarreler—somehow—will find a way to argue about your faulty decision-making methods.

2. IT'S HARD TO GET OUT OF THEIR QUARREL PRISON | PROVERBS 18:19

A quarrelsome brother regularly makes it so that there is no way out. The conversation will feel like being locked in prison with no way out. Every way you try to maneuver the conversation meets more resistance, more opposition. The picture here is of someone shaking prison bars, wishing they could get out. A quarreler finds ways to keep the conversation a quarrel.

3. QUARRELERS KEEP DRIPPING QUARRELS | PROVERBS 19:13

Drip. Drip. Drip. Drip. That is what a quarreling wife is like. They don't stop. They're disagreeable by disposition, always ready and willing to oppose. They may not always be loud or out of control. But you'll find yourself thinking, "They never stop!"

4. QUARRELERS LIKE TO BE LOUD | MATT 12:19, IS 42:2

Isaiah prophesied that when Christ comes, "He will not quarrel or cry aloud, nor will anyone hear his voice in the streets." Quarreling is rarely quiet. Quarrelers want to be heard and seen. They want to make sure other people hear their position. Jesus had a way of quietly getting out of the most heated conversations. Christ came like a lamb and remained silent even while on trial (1 Peter 2:23). Quarrelers tend to be loud.

5. QUARRELERS CRAVE A QUARREL | 1 TIMOTHY 6:4

Quarrelers don't accidentally find themselves in regular disputes, some of which may be necessary to protect the fidelity of the gospel. No, they crave it. Some people sip coffee. Quarrelers guzzle quarrels. They enjoy going back and forth, debating about words and saying, "Surely you meant *this* when you said *that*." They don't want to get to a resolution *too* quickly. They love the quarrel itself. They can find a quarrel anywhere and make a quarrel out of anything. Does it discourage or belittle a brother or sister? No matter.

It reminds me of my children going nuclear over who gets to sit where at the dinner table. There is no privilege or right involved, nothing is gained or lost. They themselves, not the subject of debate, are the real source of the quarrel. They crave it.

QUARRELING PRODUCES STRIFE AND DIVISION

Following from 1 Timothy 6:4, quarreling doesn't produce the fruit of faith, patience, and unity. It leads to division and a culture of suspicion. In Corinth the people quarreled about their favorite teacher and instead of producing love and affection for servants of God, it produced division (1 Corinthians 1:10-17). Quarreling severs the unity the church shares in Christ. People leave a quarrel divided over the quarrel rather than united around the gospel.

Like Linus in Charlie Brown, there's a little dust storm of division and suspicion that follows them.

CONCLUSION

The Bible expects us to discern quarrelsome people. When someone persists in quarreling, they ought to be met with all the care we give for other sins and immaturities. But one thing is for sure, we don't have the authority to merely say, "They're just really passionate" or "that's just how Bob is" or "that's just what happens on social media."

No, such behavior is quarrelsome. We should recognize it and avoid it (Titus 3:9).

ABOUT THE AUTHOR

Nathan Loudin is the senior pastor of Milwood Baptist Church in Austin, Texas.

What Is the Root of Quarrelsomeness and How Does It Get Fixed?

David Dunham

The Scriptures tell us that an elder is not to be quarrelsome (2 Tim. 2:24). Being quarrelsome is different from having arguments. A quarrelsome person doesn't just find conflict, he creates it, goes looking for it. He inserts himself into conflicts. Often he is a fault-finder, constantly critiquing others. Quarrelsome people view themselves as having a ministry of correction.

The apostle Paul warns against those who have an "unhealthy craving for controversy and for quarrels about words, which produce envy, dissension, slander, evil suspicions, and constant friction among people…" (1 Tim. 6:4b-5a). He states that "quarreling over words" succeeds "only in leading the listeners to ruin" (2 Tim. 2:14). The apostle is not describing someone who simply has arguments, but rather one who is characterized by them.

Yet what does this quarrelsomeness root in? Because only when we understand the root of the problem can we begin to find the solution.

WHAT IS THE ROOT OF QUARRELSOMENESS?

A quarrelsome person finds a sense of purpose and worth in arguments.

It's that sense of purpose and worth which causes problems. James clarifies that we get into quarrels precisely because of the desires in our hearts (James 4:1-2). We have fights and quarrels not because another person is wrong but because we want something that they won't give us. We fight because we have a desire to be right, and to be thought of as right, which gives us a sense of purpose. Ultimately this desire stems from pride and insecurity.

We, of course, know that pride leads to destruction (Prov. 16:18), but more pointedly pride will keep us from genuinely caring for a congregation. Where the Bible calls us to do "nothing from selfish ambition or conceit, but in humility count others more significant than yourselves" (Phil. 2:3-4), pride asserts self-importance.

Pride says that my view, my perspective, my voice, my position is most important. My views are more important than their views, and in fact my views are more important than them. Likewise, insecurity will keep us from loving because of our need to be validated.

A quarrelsome person can't ignore a wrong comment, nor can he accept critical feedback. He must justify himself and defend his views. He must be right, and he will only finally accept it if someone else affirms it. The insecure person will quarrel in order to preserve their self-image, and pressure others to reinforce that self-image.

Evaluate yourself, pastor. Do you find it difficult to resist correcting others? Is it hard to obey Romans 15:1? Are your social media accounts full of conflicts? Do you insert yourself into arguments online? Do you use other words to describe your quarrelling (like disagreement, dialogue, or discussion)? Would other people characterize you as quarrelsome?

WHAT IS THE SOLUTION?

The way forward for the quarrelsome person involves a level of humiliation. The proud and insecure heart will always want to set the terms of repentance. True change will come not simply in trying to be humble, but in being humbled.

The quarrelsome person needs a gracious authority in his life to whom he must confess his sins. Where his quarreling has been public (e.g. online), he needs to make a public confession under the guidance of such an authority.

Pastors must be held accountable, and so an elder board full of "yes-men" will not help them to grow and change. But key figures who have the wisdom, the backbone, and the love to call their pastors to repentance will.

A quarrelsome pastor is an unqualified pastor. Therefore, we need not only to evaluate ourselves, but we need others to help us. A prideful and insecure heart will destroy a ministry, but a humbled heart can serve the Lord and his church well.

ABOUT THE AUTHOR

David Dunham is pastor of counseling and discipleship at Cornerstone Baptist Church in Roseville, MI.

www.ingramcontent.com/pod-product-compliance
Lightning Source LLC
Chambersburg PA
CBHW060016050426
42448CB00012B/2775